CABIN STORIES

CABIN STORIES

THE BEST OF *DARK WINTER NIGHTS:* *TRUE STORIES FROM ALASKA*

EDITED BY

Rob Prince

UNIVERSITY OF ALASKA PRESS
Fairbanks

© 2022 by University Press of Colorado

Published by University of Alaska Press
An imprint of University Press of Colorado
245 Century Circle, Suite 202
Louisville, Colorado 80027

 The University Press of Colorado is a proud member of
the Association of University Presses.

The University Press of Colorado is a cooperative publishing enterprise supported, in part, by Adams State University, Colorado State University, Fort Lewis College, Metropolitan State, University of Denver, University of Alaska Fairbanks, University of Colorado, University of Northern Colorado, University of Wyoming, Utah State University, and Western Colorado University.

∞ This paper meets the requirements of the ANSI/NISO Z39.48-1992 (Permanence of Paper).

ISBN: 978-1-64642-331-6 (paperback)
ISBN: 978-1-64642-332-3 (ebook)
https://doi.org/10.5876/9781646423323

Library of Congress Cataloging-in-Publication Data

Names: Prince, Robert W., 1977– editor.
Title: Cabin stories : the best of "Dark winter nights" / edited by Rob Prince.
Other titles: Best of "Dark winter nights"
Description: Fairbanks : University of Alaska Press, [2022]
Identifiers: LCCN 2022014585 (print) | LCCN 2022014586 (ebook) | ISBN 9781646423316 (paperback) | ISBN 9781646423323 (ebook)
Subjects: LCSH: Alaska–Biography–Anecdotes. | Adventure and adventurers–Alaska–Anecdotes. | Dark Winter Nights (Podcast)
Classification: LCC F904.6 .C33 2022 (print) | LCC F904.6 (ebook) | DDC 979.8–dc23/eng/20220506
LC record available at https://lccn.loc.gov/2022014585
LC ebook record available at https://lccn.loc.gov/2022014586

Cover illustrations © Afishka/Shutterstock (front), MicroOne/Shutterstock (background, top), Sabrina Patrice/Shutterstock (background, bottom)

Contents

Preface

It's tough when Hollywood calls. It's very intimidating—kind of like having the most popular girl in high school ring you up out of the blue. I was utterly unprepared for it, so I was rather star-struck the morning I got a call from a Los Angeles production company. It was one of those house-hunting type shows looking for help finding people living the rustic dry cabin life in my town: Fairbanks, Alaska. Dry cabins are typically small dwellings with outhouses and no running water, and they're understandably pretty novel to people in the rest of the world.

This production company's plan was to deceive their audience by finding people here in Fairbanks who already lived in a dry cabin and have them *pretend* to be shopping for a dry cabin. Then (SURPRISE!) at the end of the episode they would pick the cabin that they were *already* living in. A number of house-hunting programs use this strategy to streamline their production process and keep costs low, especially when filming in remote locations. It turns out portraying reality is not as cost-efficient as most reality TV shows would like it to be, so they fake it.

Since I was relatively new to Alaska and looking to build my career as a professor in the journalism department of the University of Alaska Fairbanks, I agreed to help. Admittedly, I did assume there would be something in it for me. I did a little research and passed on some names to them. They were grateful and that was the last I heard from them. Even though they ended up using some of the people I found for their show, they never acknowledged my help in any way.

I was not used to being exploited and I really didn't like it. Not only had I helped them with their business for free, with zero recognition of my effort, but I had inadvertently helped them portray a caricature of life in Alaska that panders to what cable TV audiences want to see and not what life is really like here. It was at that point that I decided that if people were so interested in what life in Alaska was like, then we should have *Alaskans* sharing true stories from Alaska with the world and not outsiders exploiting our great state and broadcasting made-up nonsense.

That is how my idea for a Fairbanks-based storytelling program was born. I called it *Dark Winter Nights: True Stories from Alaska*. I assembled a small team of friends and students, and we put together our first live storytelling program in April 2014. We held the event in a modest theater that seats 330 people and ended up drawing a crowd of about 220. Seven months later, after the word had gotten out a little more, we packed that venue well beyond capacity. People were sitting in the aisles—and these were Alaskans who already had a pretty good idea of what life in Alaska is like. The next spring we moved to a 1,200-seat venue in town and have never looked back. In 2021 the *New York Times* called *Dark Winter Nights* the best winter podcast for storytelling lovers, and in 2022 National Public Radio's *Weekend Edition* aired three of our stories on their nationally broadcast program. Who are these people with amazing stories that have drawn such incredible national attention? Regular Alaskans, many of whom you are about to meet in this book. That's the beauty of life in Alaska. Adventure will find you up here whether or not you are looking for it. I hope you enjoy this selection of stories that we tell up here in Alaska on dark winter nights.

CABIN STORIES

Is It Kosher?

ALEXANDRA DUNLAP

Alexandra is an example of why I sometimes wonder why we bother to put so much work into recruiting and coaching storytellers. At every show we ask people to submit their name if they would like to tell a story that night live on stage with no rehearsal or coaching. Then we pick one person to be our audience storyteller that night. Often these stories are just as strong as the storytellers we coached, making me question what service I really provide for the show—and Alexandra's story is one such example. She told this story in front of hundreds of people, off-the-cuff and with zero coaching, at our April 2015 live event.—Rob Prince

Before I tell you my story, there's some background information you need to know. I was born and raised in Los Angeles, California. In my early twenties (okay . . . nineteen), I met this adorable red-head at a party my sister was throwing. I fell in love with him and we got married. At the time I was not aware that before you marry a boy from Alaska, you should prepare a prenuptial agreement to ensure that you don't ever have to move back to Alaska.

He was very sweet to me. When we were first married we lived in Denver for a couple years, so I actually got to see what it looks like when snow falls from the sky, but eventually we did move up to Alaska. I grew up in L.A.—freeway onramp noise at night, helicopters, arms fire (from handguns), and crack pipes on the front lawn. I wasn't quite prepared for some aspects of life in Alaska.

At the time of this story we had been in Alaska about two and a half years. It was a lovely spring morning, not much ice left on the ground. As I walked my children to the school bus across our fairly large piece of property, I noticed what appeared to be a dead moose in the back of one of our paddocks. To protect my children (or myself with the pretense of protecting my children), I nervously stepped around the moose, keeping as much space as possible between us and it. I got them to the bus stop then immediately came home and called the Department of Fish and Game.

They said, "Ma'am, we need you to go over to the moose and see if any of your neighbors poached it."

I said, "I'm not comfortable with that."

"Well, you have to do it, ma'am—just go look for any gunshot wounds." "I'm from L.A.!" I said. "I can handle gunshot wounds!" I walked over, making a concerted effort not to make eye contact with a dead animal. I looked at the body; from what I could see, there were no gunshot wounds. I called Fish and Game back and told them what I'd seen.

Fish and Game said, "Okay. Well, your property, your cleanup."

"Okay." So then I called Animal Control.

They said, "Ma'am, we need you to go over to the body . . ."

I cut them off, "I already went over to the body!"

"What did you do?"

"I checked it for gunshot wounds to make sure none of my neighbors poached it!"

"Okay, ma'am, is there a dog's tail twitching underneath it? From what you can see, did it land on somebody's dog?"

"Well . . . I don't think so?"

And they said, "It's your property; it's your problem."

So then I called my daddy and asked if I could come back home to L.A.

He said, "No! It's your property; it's your problem!"

"Dad! You're in L.A.!"

"Your husband is your property," he said.

And I said, "Ohhhhhh, okay! I got it!" Then I called my husband at work. I had to tell him the story a few times because by then I was shaking pretty bad. There was no way I could handle this anymore.

Because this is Fairbanks, he went up to his boss and told him, "There's a dead moose in my yard. I have to go home and process it."

And his boss said, "Oh, yeah—go." Who knew a dead moose is an acceptable excuse for getting out of work?

My husband came home and called a couple of his friends. They also got off work and came over. After having a look at the moose, my husband told me quite gently that moose don't tend to wear their heads backwards—it had probably snapped its neck in our fence, which was partially bent over on top of the body.

We began to contemplate what had happened to this moose. My husband thought the moose was inexperienced; it seemed fairly young and this may have been its first year on its own. My oldest son thought maybe it had just made some bad moose decisions. Like it had been out partying all night with friends and one moose said to the other moose, "Dude, I bet you can't get through that fence . . ." I said, "Well, they're not surfers. I think he would have said 'Man, I bet you can't get through that fence.'" However it happened, though, it obviously turned out to be a bad idea for the moose.

In the end we decided to rule its death a suicide because not only am I an L.A. girl, I'm a *Jewish* L.A. girl. While I'm not a rabbi, I believe a moose that committed suicide is kosher. I also believe young moose should not let other young moose make stupid decisions.

Birdshot

ALYSSA ENRIQUEZ

*There are a lot of things to love about Alaska but, like anywhere, we have
our own struggles. Alyssa's story is a great blend of the wonders of Alaska
with the deep struggles life up here can bring. She shared this story at our
November 2014 live event in Fairbanks.—Rob Prince*

So it started with a boy. Doesn't it always start with a boy? We met
online in 2007 and five years later he came to San Francisco to visit
me for about three weeks. After that he invited me to come up to
Nome, Alaska, and I said, "Sure." I knew nothing about Nome and
had never even wanted to know about Nome.

I booked a flight and packed about ten bags of clothes—none
of which were useful once I got to Nome. So June 24, 2012, as the
plane descends for landing I am looking out the window and there
are absolutely no trees. That kind of blew my mind. Nome is up in
northwest Alaska on the Bering Sea. It's arctic tundra and there
are no trees. I was completely awestruck with the beauty of the
land before I even met the people.

I was welcomed by about ten friends and family members of
my friend Isaac, who soon proved to be somebody I would grow to
love and cherish. The first thing we did was drop off our bags and
then set a fishing net from a flat-bottomed boat on the Bering Sea.
Isaac's dad, cigarette hanging out of his mouth, tossed me a life
jacket and said, "Here put this on, you might need this!" So we're

on the boat and we're bumping along and I was still in my leather boots and my leather jacket, thinking, "Okay, whatever!" So we set the net and then headed out to the family home, about four miles outside of Nome proper. I had caribou burgers for the first time and I had only been in Alaska for about an hour. I was thinking, "Heck, I could dig this!"

Then some of Isaac's friends came by. Somebody tossed me a pair of rubber boots that were about three sizes too big and a raincoat. I put them on. It was raining. We headed back out to check the net. I had never seen so many fish in a net in my life. Actually, I had never really gone fishing either, so it was kind of this amazing moment of "Wow, I get to eat these tonight!" We came home and we fried them up. That was the moment when I thought I could really, really enjoy living in Alaska.

One stipulation of me coming to Nome was that I would get a job, and boy, did I get a job! I ended up on Little Diomede Island: population about sixty. The high school there was sliding into the ocean, so we were jacking it back up. I would sit with the hydraulic jack for about twelve hours pumping it up and pumping it up and thinking, "What the heck did I get myself into?!" That was also when Isaac decided to tell me he loved me—as I'm jacking up this high school and I'm covered in dirt . . . I looked at him and said, "You're absolutely crazy, but okay, I love you too!"

We were on the island for about eleven days. It was supposed to only be nine, but we were stuck for two extra days due to bad weather. Finally the weather cleared and we were able to fly back to Nome. As we were heading back, the pilot banked the helicopter so we could watch some gray whales swimming in the water. I was thinking to myself, "Whoa, this is so cool! I love Alaska!" A little further along we saw some bears running along the coast, and once again I thought, "Whoa, I love Alaska!"

By the time we got back to Nome I had decided to move to Alaska. When I told Isaac and his family they said, "Okay, cool!" Then I had to call my parents to tell them I was moving to Alaska. I flew back to San Francisco to finish up my work and pack ten boxes.

I moved to Fairbanks, Alaska, without ever having been here. It turned out to be a very tough winter—it snowed until June. I ended up going back to Nome for the summer under the stipulation that I would have a job, only this time I took one at Subway—no more pumping jacks.

One day I took a day off and Isaac and I went fishing. We canoed down the Pilgrim River. We caught a bunch of fish and were cooking them on a bed of fresh willows when maybe ten yards away we saw bears in the river—also eating their dinner. I really loved Alaska at that point. It was the only day I had ever skipped out of work because I had so much fun fishing. I never thought I'd hear myself say that: I took a day off to go fishing. I fell in love with Alaska, but I also fell in love with a community and Isaac's family.

This summer I went back up to Nome to work. Isaac and I were celebrating our second anniversary on the Fourth of July and we decided to go on a canoe trip. It was really fun paddling down the Nome River. Two days later, back at home, we got a phone call from Isaac's youngest brother. "We have one less family member." We were dumbfounded. We looked at each other, and hugged. Then I said a quick prayer for strength and we headed out to the family house. Isaac's younger brother had shot himself in the entryway of his parents' home.

I didn't know what my place was in my Alaskan family until that moment—until I couldn't take away the pain I was watching this family go through. The only thing I knew to do was to help in practical ways. In rural Alaska there isn't a cleanup crew to come take care of everything when something like this happens, so Isaac's mother took on much of that role. The next day I cleaned up. While we were all grieving, I wrote a poem. I'd like to share it with you.

Birdshot

The sound of birdshot, rolling across the blood-stained wood floor,
Refuses to leave my memory.
Metallic iron scent lingering, even after two coats of paint.
Oppressive summer sun, so foreign to this land.
Beads of sweat as my hands rhythmically scrub away bits of a
    person I once knew and cared for.
Ten hours and I still can't bring myself to stop scrubbing.
I leave only to scream, to cry, to let it sink in.

I sink into the late-evening dew-soaked earth.

My knees are dirty and my hands know the only thing that feels safe is to help.

I ask, "Did you have enough to eat? Here, I'll make you a sandwich." Strangers hug, awkward words escaping, while the whispers swirl.

Was it intentional? They ask me, but I am numb.

"I don't know" I plead with my eyes, and I shrug.

I barricade myself in memories, not my own.

The sound of the scanner, and the scent of old photographs is hopeful.

I smile and laugh until I am crying.

His father stands silently behind me, and places a warm hand on my shoulder.

But I cannot turn around.

I do not have adequate words to express that I'm sorry, because "sorry" is not sufficient.

The sniffles say enough.

Finally I turn around, but he's gone.

And there beside me sits a picture.

A successful hunt.

Pride on his face and Amos is nearly eleven, and I hear the sound of birdshot . . .

Rolling across the blood-stained floor.

What We Do for Our Grandkids

ED SHIRK

Ed was another friend of mine I recruited for the show because he was a great storyteller and a genuinely kind and generous man—as this story demonstrates. Sadly, he passed away in 2021, but we were glad our recording of his story could be used in the celebration of his life. One of the greatest honors in producing this show is being able to save these stories and pass them on to future generations. Ed told this story live on stage during the Midnight Sun street festival in Fairbanks in 2016.—Rob Prince

This story began in February 2000 when my son, his wife, and their three children decided that they wanted to go to Hawaii. As the grandparents, we were aware that they were going to need a babysitter for their Chihuahua Zeke. Zeke is kind of a high-strung dog and whenever there's a change in what's going on around him, he gets pretty excited. We had a family friend with an eighteen-year-old daughter named Jodi who volunteered to stay at my son's house and take care of Zeke.

About 7:00 the first night she was by herself, Jodi called us, sobbing. "Zeke won't come back in the house!" Now, what you need to know is that Zeke is a tiny Chihuahua, it was February, and it was thirty degrees below zero that night. There was a very limited amount of time to rescue Zeke before he turned into a popsicle.

I said to my wife, "Honey, what do you want to do? Do you want to go up there?" She said, "It's thirty below, I'm not going anywhere!"

"Oh, come on!" I protested. "Not even for the grandkids?"

"Nope, not even for the grandkids."

So I got on my heavy-duty overalls and my winter boots, jumped in my pickup, and headed out on Chena Hotsprings Road to Zeke's house. I soon discovered that Zeke was underneath a little storage shed at the side of the house. I got down on my knees and called to him to come out. Well, Zeke doesn't like me, so that didn't accomplish much. Once or twice he kind of acted like he was going to come, but didn't. He remained under the corner of the shed, shivering as you'd expect a Chihuahua to do at thirty below zero. I found an old piece of metal pipe and went around to the corner of the shed closest to Zeke. I banged the pipe on the frozen ground and managed to create a large enough opening that I could reach my hand up under the shed. At the same time, Jodi was up at the front of the shed looking, shining a flashlight underneath. Every time I got close to Zeke he'd scoot further under the shed. I made a couple wild grabs, but couldn't get hold of him.

At that point I was out of ideas. Then I thought, "Oh! I know! Zeke loves my son's wife!" So I called her in Hawaii and I said, "Zeke is under the shed and he won't come out. Can you try calling him over the phone?"

I ended up lying on the frozen ground with a cell phone in one hand and a flashlight in the other while my daughter-in-law said, "Zekey! Zekey! Come here, Zekey!" At first it looked like it would actually work. He scooted closer and closer—but he stayed just out of reach, and eventually he retreated back to the far corner.

His shivering was getting worse. At this point he was almost convulsing. This was one cold little Chihuahua. I called the animal shelter and asked them to bring out one of their long dog poles—the ones with the loops on the end of them. I found out they wouldn't; they would only come out if the dog had hurt someone. I may have been a little angry at that point. I may have said something along the lines of "I'm a taxpayer in the borough and you won't even come over here and help me?" I may not have been quite that polite . . .

At any rate, then I called the state troopers. Now, that had to be one of the funniest phone calls they ever got. I asked them to make Animal Control come over and help me. They told me they could not do that. They said they might have a dog pole and volunteered to go out into their shop and look for it. "If it's still there, you can use it!" After a few minutes of looking, they informed me that they couldn't find it. Well, at least *they* tried.

I went back out and shined the light under the shed again. Zeke was so cold at this point that he was no longer shivering. His eyes were starting to kind of glaze over. I thought, "I don't really like this dog, but my grandkids will really feel bad if he doesn't make it, so I've got to do something." I grabbed a stick, shoved it in there, and poked Zeke. He didn't even respond. He was so cold that he was past caring. Then I got an idea. I ran into my son's garage and grabbed his cordless Skilsaw. I went into the shed and moved everything away from the corner above where Zeke was hiding. "I'll cut a hole through the floor of the shed and then I'll be able to grab him." I thought. "And if he raises his head while that saw is cutting above him . . . well, at least I'll have done my best." So I got in there and cut a hole, then pulled back the wood so that I could grab Zeke. There he was—unconscious. I pulled him out and took him in my arms. Jodi ran in the house and got a towel. We wrapped him up and tried to get him warmed up. I said, "Jodi, you've been through enough. I'm just going to take Zeke home and Grandma and I will take care of him. You just watch the house."

So I took Zeke and we headed back to my place. Partway home, Zeke started shivering again and his eyes looked like they were focusing again. By the time I got home, this dog was going through the stages of hypothermia in reverse. I took him inside and my wife bundled him up in a blanket and held him. I heated up some milk on the stove. I put a saucer of milk on the couch and Zeke started drinking. I reached down to pet him and said, "Zeke, I'm so glad you made it!"

And Zeke went, "*Rrrrrrr!!!*" and bit my finger, drawing blood.

The Fastest Twelve-Year-Old White Boy

GLENNER ANDERSON

Glenner is a legend in radio broadcasting in Fairbanks, so it was a treat to have him on stage to share a story from his childhood in Alaska. This story shows that Alaskan dads can be as empathetic and caring as dads anywhere. He told this story live on stage at our April 2015 live event in Fairbanks.—Rob Prince

In summer of 1975, when I was twelve years old, my sister Linda, who was about twenty-four, invited me to stay with her for the summer in Juneau. I was very excited. At the time she and her then husband Sid were renting a home about fifteen miles outside of Juneau near Auke Bay. Auke Bay is a stretch of beach about a mile long with about seven or eight little streams that flow into the ocean. Around each of these streams is a little picnic area. It is beautiful. I would hang out there and play with the neighborhood kids. We did what kids do—made bow and arrows and spears; rode bikes. We knew all the trails around Auke Bay.

About midsummer my parents came to visit. My father taught me how to hunt, how to fish, how to build snow caves. He raced motocross. He raced motorboats. He worked for the Department of Transportation back in the day. He was a very smart man, so I was very excited he was coming.

When my parents arrived we all headed to the store and got all the trimmings for a picnic on Auke Bay. We could have chosen the picnic area nearest the house. That would have been nice and easy. "No, no, let's go to the one at the other end of the beach," they decided. I was out riding my bike, so they told me what time to be there. I parked my bike at the first camp area and walked down the trail to where the family picnic was going to be. It was about half a mile down the trail and I had to pass over several little ten-foot wooden walking bridges, crossing each stream. We had a great picnic, sat out by the ocean, did some fishing, had some fun. It was a rare beautiful, sunny day in Juneau.

Afterward Mom and Dad asked me if I wanted a ride back. I decided, "No, I'll walk back. I left my bike at the end, so I'll walk back to my bike." Twelve years old, I was Mr. Independent. So they packed up all the gear, headed back to the car, and left for the house. I started walking back up the trail. When I got a couple picnic sites from the end I started to see that a few trashcans had been knocked over. "Kids," I thought.

I didn't smell danger. Passed another campsite . . . saw more mayhem. Now I noticed that a couple of the trashcans were kind of squished. This hadn't been done by kids I wanted to hang out with this summer . . . I was a good kid, so I didn't want any trouble. I started thinking about what I would say when I ran into these kids. "Hey, cool, man, you guys are far out!" It was 1975 after all . . . I had bell-bottoms, feathered Sean Cassidy hair. I wasn't sure if I was going to mingle with them, or if I'd just shun them like my mom would want me to do. I had this story all built up in my head . . . until I met them at the end of the trail. It wasn't a bunch of teen-agers. It was a bear, and I stumbled right on him. I saw trash lying around, looked across the picnic site, and there was a bear. A black bear. It was a pretty good-sized one. He wasn't a full-grown male, but for a twelve-year-old boy, he was big enough. I just stared at him for a second because now, in my head, I had to switch from thinking about what Mom had told me about bad kids to what Dad had told me about bears.

When I was growing up, we used to do a lot of hunting at our cabin on Healey Lake. We'd had bears come to the cabin, so I'd kind of dealt with them before—but I had always felt safe because I'd had Dad with me . . . and dogs and guns. Even Mom was a very good skeet shooter. She had her own reloader and she could really shoot, but I didn't have her there either.

People always tell you, "Bears are more curious than hostile; they're more afraid of you than you are of them." I remembered that one. I tried to keep that in my head, and I really should have. One time we had a bear at our cabin that just punctured the toilet paper rolls in our outhouse. He was so careful—he just gently bit down on both toilet paper rolls in our two-seater outhouse without knocking them off their holders. So I was hoping this would be one of those gentle bears. But then I remembered that bear had destroyed the rest of the cabin.

From what I could remember of what my dad had told me about bears, I had several courses of action open to me. I could do the curl-up-in-a-ball thing, but I thought that might be a bit premature. I should wait until he made his move; otherwise it would look pretty silly if I just lay down in a ball on the ground. Or I could do the "be bigger than the bear" thing. But at this point the bear stood up on his hind legs. I *wasn't* going to be bigger than the bear. I'd heard that if it's a black bear you're facing, you should run down a hill. Well, there was no hill. There was the ocean, which I kept in mind. I could have tried to make it to the ocean, but there was a pretty good distance between me and the water.

So I decided just to back off and head back up the trail. "There's nothing to see here, bear! It's all good!" The bear came down off his hind legs and started slowly walking toward me, so I went a little faster. I thought, "Maybe I'll just turn around, you know, like I hadn't seen the crime." Maybe he thought I was going to turn him in for mayhem or something. "No, man, your secret's safe with me! I saw nothing! I don't even know your name, where you live, nothing!" So I started walking up the trail. He also began walking up the trail. I walked a little faster up the trail. He walked up the trail a little faster, too. At this point I did the one thing you're never supposed to do around a bear: I ran. The tough Alaskan man in me ran . . . frightened. I was moving *so fast*. I was the fastest twelve-year-old boy on the planet. I mean, I was *moving*. I still remember the sound of my shoes hitting each of those bridges, those ten-foot bridges! Thump . . . Thump . . . Thump . . . Once I turned around; that bear wasn't twenty feet behind me. I was starting to panic at this point. As I ran I could hear the bear making the strangest sound I'd ever heard a bear make. It was an almost panicked groan. I looked back again and that's when I saw the whites of this bear's eyes. I'll never forget it. They were huge. He was running right behind, not ten feet behind me now, and I saw that as he was running after me, he kept glancing back over his shoulder. That's when I did the second stupidest thing you can do around a bear: I stopped. I turned and I tried to look ready for a fight, because that's what scares a bear: a boy in bell-bottoms looking like Sean Cassidy, with his fists balled up ready for a fight.

I swear to God, that bear's four legs came to a screeching halt. He looked at me and let out what sounded almost like a scream. Which was him basically saying, "What the hell are you stopping for?! It's probably still chasing us!" This is when I realized the bear wasn't *chasing* me. He saw me running from something and assumed it was something dangerous, so he was running from it, too! He looked at me and went, "Ahhhhhh! You can stay here, but I'm gone!" and he continued up the trail past me, until all I could hear was his muffled scream in the distance.

I was pretty shaken and pretty sure I'd wet myself a little. I walked back down the trail, got my bike, and headed back to the house. I burst in and said, "You'll never believe what just happened! I was chased by a bear! Well, kind of—it was a bear, and it was right behind me!" They all started laughing. Nobody believed me. I was so mad. I went outside, sat by the ocean, watched the sun set on a beautiful day, and I cried—I think partly from the stress of what had just happened, and partly because my family didn't believe me.

Then I felt a hand on my shoulder. It was my dad. He said, "Whadya say we head up there and look for that bear of yours?"

"Thanks, Dad." So Dad and I headed down the trail. We walked almost all the way, talking about everything, but saw nothing. We got to our picnic area. Nothing. He'd seen the trash around and it was obvious something had happened there. We saw something that was probably bear tracks, but no bear. We turned around and headed back. Just as we were almost home, that bear ran right across our path—right in front of us. He just looked at us and ran by. It was almost like he was still scared. I yelled, "Look, Dad! Dad!"

"I see him, I see him," he said. Dad was always the one who believed me. He was always the one to say, "We better go check it out." So thanks to my dad, I got redemption.

That's a story I still like to tell to my dad. He's older now. He's in the Pioneer's Home. He has Alzheimer's disease. So the man who used to be the smartest guy I've ever met now has the mind of a child. He's always happy, though. He's really happy. I can tell him all our stories and the best part is that now I get to tell them over and over again, and he loves to hear them every time. I can't wait until I go visit him tomorrow and say, "Hey, Dad, remember the time that bear chased me in Juneau?" And he's going to say, "Yeah, that was great!" and I'll tell the story to him all over again.

Lost at Sea

GUY SCHRODER

Guy was part of our first live event ever and, for me, rock-solid proof that we were on to something important with this storytelling thing we were trying to do. We were so amazed by his story that we brought him and his family up from Anchorage for the show—something we very rarely do. He shared his story for the first time publicly at the first Dark Winter Nights *live event in April 2014.—Rob Prince*

I want to explain to you about the western Aleutians, the water out there, and how God can just stand it up in the blink of an eye. There are whirlpools the size of large buildings. The tide of the North Pacific crashes into the Bering Sea. Fifty-foot waves will rise up out of nowhere. It's uncontrollable, magical, mystical.

It was about the middle of October and fishing was pretty good for the most part. We delivered our load to Adak Naval Base. We had all the original crew with us. Two of the guys got off the boat there at Adak. One was an engineer who ran the refrigeration, but he didn't do a very good job, so he was frustrated. It was lucky those two got off the boat there; otherwise they probably wouldn't be here today.

After we left Adak, we got into a force four hurricane. We were trying to get across Amchitka Pass so we could get back home in time for Halloween. That was the skipper's decision. We got by Semisopochnoi Island and lost our steering. The boat went sideways. I was the deck boss, so I was woken up and mustered up to the wheelhouse to talk to the skipper. At first we were listing to the port side. We were getting heavier and heavier in the water. We had 2,776 forty-pound blocks of codfish. All our freezers were full. We had 450 pots on the boat. We had *way* too much weight on the boat for this water. The boat used to be a deep fish dragger and was never properly restabilized for the type of fishing we were doing.

We were not able to keep up with the water, which was coming in faster than we could pump it, so we kept getting heavier. We got sideways. The wind was blowing over 100 miles an hour and there were fifty-foot seas. We were just getting torn apart. I got everyone suited up as fast as I could. I sent three guys to the bottom of the deck where I threw over a raft to them. I was hoping they would open it. Then I had them help me get the crane hooked up to start dumping equipment overboard, but the motors wouldn't work.

After that I don't know what happened to those three guys. I was hoping that they'd gotten in that raft, but it turns out that they didn't. If they did make it, nobody else knows about it. The other seven us did manage to get into a raft.

The engineer never suited up. He stayed in the wheelhouse and tried to keep us even keel, which was nearly impossible. His body was never found. As he was jockeying the boat back and forth, I tied a clove hitch to secure our raft to the boat. I should never have used a clove hitch around the rail, but I was so scared of losing the raft. I almost didn't get that knot untied. Once I had, we started listing to the starboard side. Next thing I knew, I lost my balance and did a face-plant right into the anchor winch—knocking out my front teeth. At that point I jumped into the water and climbed into the raft with the others.

I could see the ship's lights starting to dim. Right before those lights went out, I saw the silhouette of the mast coming right down on top of me. I thought for sure that mast was going to take us down. Luckily, it didn't. After the boat went under, we took a wave that knocked us all out of the raft. Only six of us got back into it. We lost one person on that wave. Then another wave hit us and only five of us made it back into the raft. In between those two hits, we tried to tie the door flaps of the raft closed, but it was blowing so hard we couldn't do it. So we were exposed to that side of the weather.

A third wave hit us and ripped the whole top off the raft. There was a bright strobe on the top of the raft and once it was gone, we couldn't find the raft in the darkness anymore. It was pitch black and we were in a hurricane. It's one thing to be on land in a hurricane, but in the Aleutian passes it's a whole different ball game.

There is survival equipment strapped into the inside of the raft. I made the mistake of taking the bags off the side of the raft and distributing the water and other survival equipment to the guys. We lost most of that in those waves. It was very difficult to get back into the raft after being thrown out again and again. There was a rope around the outside of the raft you could hold onto, but there was no cobweb line to help you pull yourself back in. We were thrown out of the raft over twenty times, and it took all of our strength and will to get back into the boat each time.

I spent seventeen and a half hours fighting for my life. They found us thirty-five miles away. When I finally got picked up by the helicopter, I couldn't stop crying. I was sure that the helicopter was going to crash and I'd just lost so many men I'd been fishing with.

I made a pact with God that night. I told him, "If you get me through this, I will turn my life to you." He kept his word, and I'm still trying to keep mine.

Why I Hate Camping

JAMES MENNAKER

James is another friend I recruited for our live show who ended up delivering a true gem of a story for us. As a father, I love his story because I can put myself in his dad's shoes, trying to figure out what to do in a very perilous situation with no other adult to consult with and three young boys to manage. As a dad you just have to play it by ear and do the best you can. He shared this story at our first live event in April 2014.–Rob Prince

Well, I was bummed. My whole family was bummed, actually. It was 1984 and I was ten years old. I had two younger brothers, one nine, one five, and my dad had just bought land off of 26-mile Chena Hotsprings Road. He was going to take us out there on a nice long weekend to explore the property. We had been planning this trip for a month or so. During the week leading up to it, it rained nonstop. It was one of those rainy summers that we sometimes get in Fairbanks. *Rained* is the wrong word, actually. It had *poured* for a week.

So we were all just feeling bummed. My mom especially, because she lived in a house full of four guys, and she was really excited about being able to have a long quiet weekend by herself.

The rain finally stopped the day before we were going to leave. As the skies cleared, my dad said, "It is game on! We are going tomorrow!" We were thrilled, confident we would not bothered by rain on this adventure.

So we loaded up my dad's old red and white Dodge pickup truck that he'd been driving for fifteen years. We secured the canoe on top of it and packed the canopy on the back with supplies and camping gear—everything you need for a long weekend of hiking and exploring. My dad got into the driver's seat, the three of us got into the cab, and off we went. My mom was waving, smiling, tears of joy coursing down her face—we knew that the instant we were out of sight she would turn to the pile of books she had waiting, confident that she would not be interrupted by any of us.

As we drove out to Chena Hotsprings Road, we found our turn and went down this winding, bumpy, gravelly road—the kind they still have there. We got down to the river and thought, "This looks like a great place to set up camp." I won't lie; the river was high. Definitely swollen, but it looked okay. We planned to camp there, then cross the river the next day. So we got camp set up around 4:30 p.m. Then we noticed that the river was even higher. No problem—we'd just move farther up the road. By the time we got our tent taken down, the river was noticeably higher still. So we moved substantially further up the road, got the tent up and the fire going. But again the river kept rising. At that point we decided maybe we should find another camping spot. By the time we got our tent taken down the second time and loaded it into the truck, the river had put out our fire. Haste may have been required at this point. Again we loaded up the truck, then drove back toward Chena Hotsprings Road to find a better camping spot.

As we came around a bend in the road, we saw that ahead of us the river had jumped its banks and was coming toward us. My dad sat there for a minute, wondering what he should do. He decided tire chains would probably be the best solution because chains *really* help in driving upriver . . . So he got out of the pickup and put on the chains, muttering to himself. We three were sitting in the cab thinking, "*This* is not what we were expecting."

After getting the truck all chained up, Dad said, "Okay, boys, here we go." And we started driving up the road. Well, at first it was a road; pretty soon we were driving up the river. As the water started engulfing the truck, Dad told my nine-year-old brother, who was sitting closest to the window, "Son, I want you to climb out the window and sit on the cab. When debris comes downriver at us, I want you to push it out of the way." So there's my brother John kicking his feet on the truck hood, pushing out sticks and making sure that nothing torpedoes us. And we were going! We were driving upriver! Finally . . . we started to float. My dad realized that chains *might not* be able to save him this time and shouted, "Abandon truck! It's time to go!"

So we climbed out the windows and he took the canoe off the top of the truck and set it onto the road/river. We got my brothers into the canoe, put whatever supplies we could fit into it, and started paddling up the road. The road turned into rapids and we started going up and down and around. We came to a high point where it was dry and my dad decided this would be a good place to camp and have a little break. We had a nice view of our truck disappearing under the water as we drank hot chocolate.

Then we decided we should go home, so we canoed up the road again. Finally we came to dry land. Leaving the canoe and supplies, we started the very long walk back to Fairbanks. By this time it was 10:30 p.m. or so, dark, and Chena Hotsprings Road was deserted. There was not a car in sight. Finally we came up to a general store. It was closed, but my dad wanted to make a phone call, so he pounded on the door. Pretty soon the light came on and they opened up. He explained the situation and they said, "Of course you can call."

My mother, who had been giggling to herself all day in her glorious isolation and reading mystery novels in bed, answered the phone to be greeted with, "Hi, honey. We lost the truck and we need a ride home. Love you!"

My mom came to get us and we all piled into the car. It was a *very quiet* ride home. Except for the murmurs coming from Mom, something about losing the truck and having to deal with boys . . .

A few days later we headed out to try to salvage the truck. With the help of some friends, we got a winch hooked up to it and pulled it out. We drained the truck's fluids, put new oil and gas in, and my dad drove it home. He went on to drive it for the next ten years.

And that's why I hate camping to this day.

Fishing for Chickens

JB CARNAHAN

JB is the big "except" for us at Dark Winter Nights. All of our stories have to take place in Alaska, except for JB's. His is the one story we've ever shared that didn't take place in Alaska, and I think you'll understand why when you read it. Some stories are just too tempting to let pass based on a technicality. He shared this story at our first live event in April 2014.
—Rob Prince

You know, there are people outside of Alaska who think we Alaskans are a little strange. I'm going to tell you a little story about a time a friend of mine and I took a little vacation. Then you can decide if we're strange or not. I saw nothing wrong with it.

Verne Carlson and I are old fishing buddies. A couple of years ago, he and I decided to take our wives to Hawaii. It was a big deal. It's not the sort of thing we get to do very often, so we wanted to maximize our time. Of course I took along my fishing gear, because I don't go anywhere without that, and Hawaii seemed like a good place to fish.

The minute we got our rental car and started on our way to the hotel, I noticed there were chickens everywhere! I mean really, they were everywhere, and they weighed seventy pounds! Okay, maybe just five or six. Either way, it's a fabulous place, Hawaii—you'd never starve, as long as you like chicken. We went to this place called the Plantation, I think. There was this huge lawn with bungalows all along the sides and we had a bungalow right in the center. Everybody in these other bungalows could see us.

Fortified by an adult beverage, Verne and I went exploring. We realized there was no place to fish. The shore around the Plantation was pretty rocky. So I said, "Hey, Verne, look at all these chickens! I not only have all my fishing gear, but I also brought along a can of my special bait . . . corn." Corn works great for almost anything.

"Great," he said.

"I tell you what, Verne, let's get ready," I said. We grabbed a rattan chair. Being a good Alaskan, I of course had duct tape with me. So we duct-taped each of the four legs down to create a good fighting chair. Verne settled down in the fighting chair. About this time people started popping out of their bungalows to watch us. At first they didn't know what we were doing, but they started to figure it out when I grabbed my fishing rod and loaded it up with three corn kernels.

"Are you ready, Verne?" I asked. Verne was *ready*. With a flick of his wrist, he set his first cast into the lawn. At this point we were just playing. We hadn't seen any chickens around here. Then, out of nowhere—and I mean *out of nowhere*—came the biggest chicken you ever saw in your life—*and the fight was on*. There was Verne in his fighting chair and I was right beside him, helping him every bit I could.

"Alright, down with the rod, that's it, pull up, reel down . . ." I instructed. This went on for a good ten minutes. This chicken was not happy, although I think most of the chickens there aren't happy anyway. Verne reeled the chicken closer and closer. At this point the crowd of spectators was getting larger. We were having a great time. The chicken, who was not having a great time, got about ten feet from us when he suddenly realized that all of his trouble was coming from *that man* who was holding a stick in his hand. At this point the bird took off, flying right at Verne. I didn't know they could fly! Did you? I mean, nobody told us they could fly or we might not have done this. The bird hit him right in the chest. Did I mention he was bare-chested? Probably another reason we had drawn a crowd . . . I had not duct-taped things the way I should have, apparently (Verne later maintained the whole incident was my fault), and the chair went over backwards. Verne, the chair, the chicken . . . I was trying to get the chicken; Verne, flat on his back, was trying to get up. I finally got the chicken.

Those chickens are tough! Dangerous and tough, and they don't like people holding them. So I wrestled with this chicken until the hook fell out of his beak. Fortunately it had just hooked into its beak and there was no serious injury. That would have been bad. So I took the chicken and threw him up into the air. Did he fly off toward the brush? No. He came *straight back down on Verne*. The chicken then showed his disgust with him by crapping right there on Verne's naked back before he flew off. The crowd was really enjoying itself at this point. They'd figured out, "These guys are from Alaska. This is the kind of thing they do." We had a good time with those people, although Verne ended up with a huge bruise right in the center of his chest. Man boobs with a huge bruise in the middle—not a pretty sight.

Later, after everything had settled down, we went to dinner. At the entrance to the hotel dining room this very stern man, identifying himself as the hotel manager, informed us that Hawaii's chickens are kind of like the American eagle, and not to be trifled with. Yeah, right, I'd never go fishing for eagles! He asked us not to go fishing for any more chickens or we would have to forfeit the rest of our week at the bungalow. When he finished with us, we turned into the dining room . . . to a *standing ovation*.

Dognapped

LORI SCHOENING

Lori's story still awes me to this day. Pay close attention to how long her ordeal lasted and put yourself in her young shoes. What would you have been thinking at her age over such a long time? It's also great proof that sled dogs like to run and don't need any encouragement from anyone. She shared this story live on stage during the Midnight Sun street festival in Fairbanks in 2016.—Rob Prince

I'm a lifelong Alaskan who grew up in Delta Junction. For three winters, my parents moved to Fairbanks so they could go back to school. This story takes place about thirty years ago during one of those winters in Fairbanks when I was about seven years old. My parents had made friends with a couple, Mark and Dana, who lived out in the Goldstream Valley. Their home was a typical Alaskan cabin, complete with a dog yard. Mark was a musher who had a young dog team. When he found out that I had never been on a dogsled ride, he wanted to remedy that, so he arranged it with my parents.

He picked me up from school one day and brought me out to his place. He had put a bunch of sleeping bags in the basket of the sled to keep me warm. This was the middle of winter. It wasn't super cold out, but it was definitely below zero. The dogs were already hooked up and Mark was putting his gloves on, standing behind the runners. Then he accidentally bumped a stack of bowls, probably dog dishes, with his foot, knocking them over.

The dogs were a very young team, easily spooked, and they immediately took off running. Mark didn't have ahold of the sled, so I was on my own in the basket, tearing down into the Goldstream Valley, crisscrossed by a huge network of miles and miles of trails.

I was scared. I had never been on a sled before and it felt like we were going very, very fast—especially sitting down low in that basket. Mark raced after me as fast as he could. There was no one else home, so Mark was the only one who knew that I was in this runaway dogsled. Things started to fall off the sled. As Mark fell further and further behind until I could no longer see him, I realized that I should throw *more* things off the sled so Mark could follow me. There I was, chucking stuff out of this sled hoping against hope that Mark would be able to follow this Hansel and Gretel trail and find me and his sled. The dogs would not slow down, not even to take corners.

When the dogs first took off, Mark had yelled at me to jump out, but we were racing so fast, from my perspective, that it didn't feel safe to do so. So I stayed in the basket. I screamed at the dogs to stop, but that's not the right mushing command to make a dog team stop, so they kept running. This went on for *hours*. Meanwhile, unbeknownst to me, Mark at some point came across a house and alerted the people there to watch for the little girl on a runaway dog sled. He continued after me, hoping the dogs would stick to the familiar trails they normally practiced on.

When Mark came out onto Goldstream Road, he flagged down a pickup truck and told the guy, "If you see a runaway dogsled with a little girl stuck on it, please stop the dogs!" As luck would have it, not long after that, the dogs turned onto Goldstream Road. A man in a tan pickup drove by. I remember thinking, "Oh! Maybe he's going to save me!" but he just kept going. It turned out that he was pulling forward so that he could stop ahead of me. Then he got out of his truck and ran down the embankment. My heart lifted as I realized I was finally saved. He grabbed the dogs, got them stopped, and tied them to a tree. He took me out of the sled, put me in his truck, and drove me down to the general store. The lady there was expecting me—by this time, word had gotten out that there was a child in a runaway dogsled.

I was freezing. It had been hours in this cold weather with no sleeping bags or blankets because I had thrown them all out of the sled long ago. All I had was the winter gear I was wearing.

The man carried me into the general store and set me on top of the counter. The lady behind the counter, with the best intentions, asked me, "Honey, would you like an ice cream cone?"

I said, "No, I do not want an ice cream cone. I'm so cold!" She gave me cookies instead.

Meanwhile, the man who had found me went back along the trails, found Mark, and brought him to the store.

That's when I found out there was no way to get home except *via dogsled*. Mark talked me up: "You can do this!" We went back to the sled and untangled the dogs, who had managed to get themselves all wound up. Mark had picked up most everything I'd thrown out, so he put it all back in the basket. He taught me how to stop the dogs in case something happened . . . *again*. Then, after he was standing with *both feet* on the runners and *both hands* on the sled, I got back inside. He mushed me back to his house and then took me home.

I haven't been a big dogsledder since.

Seeing You

MELISSA BUCHTA

*Melissa is among the first students I ever had when I came to teach at
the University of Alaska Fairbanks. She is a truly wonderful person and a
fabulous storyteller. It was an honor to have her on our show to share her
unique perspective on growing up in Alaska. She told this story at our first
live event in April 2014.—Rob Prince*

Let me just start by saying I love Alaska. I really do. I loved growing
up here, I love living here, and when I say that living in our state
is like living in those travel brochures that we pass around to get
all the tourists to come up here, it's true. Our state really does look
like that. I love it a lot, but it can be really difficult living here for
someone who is partially blind like me. I am legally blind. In my
case this means I'm not "sighted" enough for the sighted people
but I'm not "blind" enough for the blind people either. I live in this
really weird gray area.

When you grow up in this state, you do what everybody does:
you go on road trips. Road trips are great. You can bond with your
family, collect lots of awesome memories, but up here you mostly
go on a road trip to see the wildlife and the awesome scenery. A
lot of that is lost on someone who can't see . . . Did you know that
blind people get into National Parks for free? That's really great,
but think about it for a second. Really, what's a blind person going

to do in a national park? Here in Alaska everyone's like, "Oh, wow, look at McKinley–it's so beautiful! Look at Denali–it's so great!" I can't touch Denali. Denali's not going to say something. If I go, "Hey, Denali, how's it going?" Denali is not going to respond, "I'm doing fine, how are you?" That's not going to happen. I can't go to Yellowstone and touch Old Faithful either. I can't even get very close to Old Faithful. I can hear it, so I guess that's pretty cool. I've never been to the Grand Canyon, but I'm pretty sure that would also be lost on me. It's deep. Yay . . . fantastic . . . can we go get some tacos?

Seeing the wildlife is another big part of road trips here. All the beautiful wildlife. You've got your moose, your seals, your puffins, your polar bears, your brown bears, your wolves. When I was a kid we'd bring our binoculars on these road trips. My parents loved going down to Seward because it is so lush and gorgeous. They'd go, "Oh, look at the eagles! Look at the Dall sheep standing up there on the mountains–they're so beautiful!" And we'd pull over at over-looks to see belugas. My mom would hold these giant binoculars up to my face and try, in vain, to point my head where she thought the wildlife was. My dad and my brother, out of sheer embarrassment and/or pity, would just kind of sidestep away . . . People would come up and tap my dad on the shoulder and go, "Do you know that woman? It looks like she's abusing her child."

"No, no, she's just trying to see the belugas, like everybody else," he'd say.

At some point I decided I was sick of having my neck wrenched around by my mother and I was tired of my parents being so dis-appointed that I couldn't see anything, so I started to lie. Why not? Everybody would be happier. So whenever we'd see an eagle or a Dall sheep or a bear, I'd put my binoculars up to my face and go, "*Wow*! That's amazing! It's so cool!" But I couldn't really be that spe-cific about what I was seeing. I couldn't say, "Look at it reach into that stump!" because they would say, "That's a boulder." "Right, but the bear!" I'd say. So I would pretend to see all these things while viewing stock footage from the Discovery Channel in my head. I mean, I know what a bear looks like!

One day during our annual summer road trip we ended up in Seward. Seward, Alaska, is a little harbor town. All the wildlife boats and cruises go out of there. As we got on a boat I was super excited to see a whale. I love orca whales—I think they're beautiful and amazing creatures. Two hours went by. We saw seals and puffins; we saw dolphins; we even saw a bear. It was a great day and we were lucky to see all this wildlife. We saw glaciers, which are easy for me to see because glaciers don't move very fast and they make noise sometimes, which is nice. Glaciers: the most accessible of Alaskan scenery . . . if you're blind.

As the boat excursion continued I decided that instead of feeling upset and sad about not seeing all these animals, I would just enjoy this cruise in my own way. So I stood at the bow of the boat and held onto the railings, feeling the cold water there on my hands. I felt the boat going up and down, up and down, and rocking from side to side. I was one of the few people on the boat lucky enough not to get seasick. So I enjoyed that feeling. I looked at the rock formations as they drifted in and out of the mist. I felt the wind go through my hair. The whole experience was beautiful and I was really enjoying myself. I thought, "Even if I don't see a whale, I've had an incredible day."

We were about to go back to the harbor when the captain received a radio call from another ship that there was a pod of orcas in a nearby cove, so we pulled up there. The captain said, "If we see whales, don't scream and point because you'll scare them away." So we were all quiet as we stood against the railings of the big triple-decker boat. And then we saw them—a pod of orca whales was just hanging out in this cove. When they disappeared under the water, the captain shut the boat engine off and we all became *really* quiet, just waiting, not knowing what might happen next. I stood there with my binoculars thinking about whales. I'd just seen *Free Willy*, so I was playing those images in my head, anticipating another real-life disappointment.

The whales resurfaced and surrounded our boat. And right in front of me this beautiful, black, proud dorsal fin came slowly up out of the water. I can see to a distance of about three feet before my vision starts to get really blurry. I could see this whale *right in front of me.* I could see the white marks above its eyes and on its belly. I could see its tail . . . and I just stood there, holding onto the railing *so* tight that my knuckles turned white. I was afraid that if I moved or made a sound the whale would disappear. But it didn't.

The two of us were just *there*, in one another's space, each sensing and regarding the other. I can remember thinking, "Wow. Finally, I'm here . . . *We're* here together." I looked at the whale and I whispered, so that no one else could hear, "Thank you for letting me *see* you."

Granted, the next day I was back to lying to my parents about seeing wildlife. I regularly lie to my parents about this to this day, actually. We've just kind of come to accept it. It's our thing.

Your Average Pilot

MICHAEL DAKU

Mike is another friend I recruited to tell a story on Dark Winter Nights *because he's a great guy and a whole ton of fun to spend time with. I'm so grateful I approached him to tell a story on our show because otherwise I likely would have never heard about his incredible experience flying in remote Alaska. He told this story at our November 2014 live event in Fairbanks.—Rob Prince*

One day a friend of mine and I decide to fly to a certain fishing spot we've had our eye on. So we have our maps, we're flying north, and we have a general idea of where this place should be. We're looking around, looking around, looking around, and we're like . . . "well, crap, we can't find the place." I decide we'll just turn around and head home. Well, you know how sometimes fate strikes at the wrong time? I start to turn to the left but I just happen to look over my shoulder behind me and I think I see an airstrip back there along the river. I wonder if that's the place? So we go check it out. Of course we're fat, dumb, and happy, so we go over there, make a pass over the airstrip, and you know what? I think this is the place!

As we're coming in, we see a hill with spruce trees on our left. The river parallels the airstrip, *majorly* overgrown with grass and weeds, on the right side and then curves left to run along the end of the runway. The situation looks . . . well, it looks *okay*. I have practiced a lot of short field takeoffs and landings, so I feel fairly confident I can handle this challenging runway. I can land that plane very, very slow and very, very short. We do one more pass and I decide it looks good. We're going to go for it. We line up on the runway and go ahead and land. As we bump our way through the rollout, there's all this high grass and the prop is shredding it like a giant weed whacker. But everything is cool and we come to a stop. Okay! Good deal—we're here!

Turns out we have found the right location. We have a great time fishing for a few hours before we finally we decide we're ready to leave. And that's when I hear the voice. You know how sometimes in the back of your head you have a little nagging voice? Mine is saying, "I don't know if I should have come to this place." But it's late in the day now and we have to get the hell out of here.

So I decide okay, what we're going to do is set up for a classic short field takeoff. This is a small aircraft and any time you're flying small aircraft you're really concerned about weight. So I say to my friend, "Look, do you have to go to the bathroom? Literally . . . go now! You know that peanut butter and jelly sandwich you have left over? Throw it out!" Right? I mean, this is how concerned with weight you are.

So we have the plane at the very end of the strip. We've basically turned it around and pushed the tail back into the weeds—literally, the butt end of the airplane is sticking out into the weeds. Okay, so we've maximized our runway length and we're set. Before we take off, we walk up and down that airstrip two abreast to make sure there aren't any holes, logs, or anything else we might hit, and it looks good. I also put a soda can down on the left side of the airstrip. I say to myself, "Okay, this is our 'Go/No Go' point. If I don't have enough speed at this point, we're not flying; well have to figure out some other way out of here."

We get in the plane and start her up. The procedure for a short field takeoff is that you give it full power with the brakes on, make sure everything looks good, and then release the brakes and charge the runway. It's a little intimidating because you're standing still at full power, so the engine is roaring and the airplane is bucking. I let go of the brakes and here we go! I pull the yoke back a little bit and we're rumbling down, rumbling down. I'm watching my speed indicator and see the pop can coming up. Okay, we're ready.

I begin to rotate up and we just start to climb out when suddenly it feels like the hand of God and *boom*! It hits us. Big wind. A huge wind shear shakes us and then the world stops. One of the things you don't want to hear if you are a pilot is this sound: *EEEEEEEEEEEEeeeeeeeeee*! That's the stall horn. What the stall horn tells you, in pilot lingo, is you've exceeded the airplane's angle of attack. Basically, you're climbing too steeply and you're about to fall out of the sky. They tell you in pilot training that to stop the stall you push the nose of the airplane down. But when you're as low to the ground as we are, it goes against everything in your body to push the nose over and point back down toward earth. What's going to happen is you're going to basically nose-dive in and that's going to hurt real bad.

When I relive this moment now, I can remember that time seemed to stand still when I heard that stall horn go off, and I said to myself—and I was actually chuckling at the time because it's kind of weird the things you think about—"Hmm . . . so this is how people die in a plane crash." I swear that's what I said to myself. The other very, very interesting thing was that my life actually did flash in front of me. As that stall horn came on and I realized what was happening, I saw my life go by basically like the negatives of a film. It went, "chick, chick, chick . . ." in about ten-year increments. I can't remember any specifics, but I saw etchings of life events from each decade.

I do push the nose over. As we come in, I'm able to kind of flatten out the glide path. We veer left over the end of the runway and the river is now on our right. To our left are a bunch of boulders and rocks. When we hit the ground we sheer the landing gear off on the rocks and the right wing clips the river, but we finally come to a halt. The prop is ripped off, the landing gear is gone, and we come to a position with the nose pointing way down. I look over at my friend, who is kind of slumped over, and I think, "Oh, my God, he's broken his neck! This is not going to be good." Fortunately it turns out he's only a little shaken.

We're literally so close to the river that if we try to open the right door, my friend will fall right in. But we're able to get out of the plane and try to contact someone to rescue us. We turn on the emergency locating transmitter, which broadcasts an emergency signal and allows rescuers to track down your location. We also try making mayday calls on the radio. After about half an hour of this, suddenly the voice of God is heard over the radio: "Aircraft in distress, this is Northwest 85. Go ahead." Well, this turns out to be a Northwest Airlines pilot going over the North Pole. I explain our predicament. He calls Anchorage air traffic control, and they send out the Civil Air Patrol, and one of our "local agencies" to come and get us.

About seven hours pass before the local agency comes out to get us with a helicopter. There are two people in the cockpit, the pilot and another person. They ask for paperwork from the airplane, but it's kind of strange because other than that they don't say *anything* to us. So, we're *wup wup wup wup wup wup* all the way back to Fairbanks at tree-top level, landing at their facility in Fairbanks. But here's the thing: *there still isn't a word spoken to us.* My friend and I are looking at each other like, "Wow, this is really bizarre, you know, what's going to happen next?" The pilot shuts down the helicopter. We hear the engine spool down. These two guys look at us . . . and then they just *walk away.* I'm expecting Rod Serling to pop up from behind a bush and go, "Consider this . . . two pilots. One an average pilot . . ." Right? It was just totally bizarre.

Sometime later I was reading an issue of *Private Pilot* magazine that had to do with the average total hours of flying experience pilots had when they got into their first accident. I suddenly stopped short and thought, "Wait a second, how many hours?" I went to get my logbook. Sure enough, I had hit it almost right on the nose: 400 hours. There it is. There's your average pilot.

The View from Below

RICHARD COLEMAN

Falling through ice has been a lifelong fear of mine and I assumed it meant guaranteed death. That's why I was so amazed to meet Richard and find out he personally had fallen through river ice and survived. It's hard to think of many more classically northern nightmares than that. But that's just where his story begins. He shared this story live on stage at our first live event in April 2014.–Rob Prince

I have an old Athabascan friend—we'll call him Howard—I've known for fifty years. He lives across the Tanana River from Fairbanks. I like his Alaska Native lifestyle, so over the years I've given him a hand when I can. One day not too long ago, he called to ask me to bring my little boat down to his camp and help him slide his skiff into the river. It was springtime and the river ice had gone out. Not many ice cubes were coming down the river, so I figured it would be okay. I've done this type of thing before, so I thought to myself, "How much trouble can I get into? The ice is out, it's gone, and it's a nice sunny day." So I towed my boat down to the river and put in at Chena Pump Landing. I motored down to Howard's place on the south side of the Tanana River. It doesn't make any difference if the Tanana River is low and slow, high and fast, or frozen: it's always a semi-dangerous place, and if you don't do things just right, things go wrong.

I got to his camp and there was Howard standing on the bank with his bags packed, ready to go to town. He'd been waiting for thirty days for the ice to go out. We got a couple poles and pried his skiff free from the ground where it had frozen. He got on the back of the skiff and pushed and I went to the front and pulled on the towrope. It broke free and we started dragging this skiff down to the shore. There was still a lot of shore ice.

One minute we were sliding this boat out on the shore over the ice, and then all of a sudden I was looking up at a hole in the ice—and it was going away from me fast. That water was so cold my mind would only register, "Holy crap, it's cold!" Over and over I said that to myself. I knew I had to concentrate and do something, but it was hard to overcome "Holy crap, it's cold!"

In the winter the water gets very clear, so as I was looking up at the ice, I could clearly see the hole moving away from me, I could see air pockets, and I could see a lot of detail beneath the ice. I told myself I had to do something because I was moving downriver fast. I started swimming, trying to make it back to that hole. Then I realized the boat rope I'd been pulling was still in my hand. At that moment my brain switched from "Holy crap, it's cold" to "Hang onto the rope!" I concentrated on the rope and pulled my way back until I could pop my head up out of the hole in the ice. I'd only been in the water ten or fifteen seconds but already I had no muscle control. The cold had taken everything out of me. I couldn't pull myself up out of the water. Howard, knowing he wouldn't be able to reach over and drag me out, took an oar and shoved the boat over so that I was wedged between it and the ice around the hole. This gave me something to push off of and I managed to climb out of the water.

I survived that ordeal, although it took awhile for the panicky feeling to go away. But it wasn't very cold out, it was sunny, and I had a dry jacket I'd left hanging on a bush, so I stripped off my shirt, put on a dry one and that jacket, and started feeling better. Howard had his cabin all locked up, his stove was off, and he was ready to go to town, so I decided we should just keep going. I said, "Well, Howard, I'm feeling better. It's only two miles up to the boat landing. I can make that. Let's just take off."

We slid his boat into the water and got the motor running. I did the same thing with my boat and away we went—up the Tanana River in a couple of open boats. Immediately I began to feel good—almost glowing—as I felt how happy I was to be alive. It was dawning on me how close a call I'd had. I didn't yet realize there was something wrong with me.

Both of us got our boats up to the landing. Howard wanted to take his boat up the Chena River to town, so he gave me a wave and headed off. I turned my boat into the landing and drove it about halfway out of the water. As I stood up to get out of the boat, I fell over backwards onto the rocks and partly into the water. When I woke up sometime later, I knew I'd been unconscious: my legs were in the river and my top half was out of the water. There was nobody around. I checked myself out and decided nothing was broken. I got in my truck and turned the heater on. As I started to warm up I felt better, so I got out again, loaded my boat, and drove home, running the heater the whole way. I told my wife what had happened, but there was no drama: over the years she's gotten used to things like this. I got dry, changed clothes, and worked in the yard the rest of the day.

The next morning as I was sitting on the toilet, reaching over to get some toilet paper, my right arm just went 180 degrees off into the blue. It wouldn't do anything I wanted, and my left side was paralyzed. My wife raced me to the emergency room. The doctors quickly diagnosed me: I'd banged my head, had internal bleeding, and the pressure was building up in my head. They told me they had to get me to Anchorage. Within minutes they had me on a jet to Providence Hospital in Anchorage. The doctors there kept me in a cold room, observing me. This whole while—four days—I was unconscious. When I came to, I thought my youngest son had just walked in the door, come to take me home. I was really upset and madder than hell because I thought I'd just arrived and Providence was kicking me out because nothing could be done for me even though they had done a lot to stabilize my situation. My son calmed me down and drove me back to Fairbanks.

But I was far from recovered. I was bedridden, and my head was in really bad shape. I was having hallucinations and I thought I was losing my mind. My wife rushed me to my doctor in Fairbanks. He looked at my chart and said, "You're not losing your mind; you're having drug withdrawals." Apparently they had given me so much dope at Providence that I was suffering from withdrawal. Come to find out that during those four days in Anchorage, I'd gotten violent, and because I was so big the nurses couldn't handle me; everyone was afraid of me. So they called my wife at the hotel and asked her what to do and she said, "Give him more dope."

So that's what happened. In the end I was down for two months. When I finally felt pretty good, I called Howard. He hadn't heard the story and had no idea what had happened to me. I asked him, "Howard, do you always put the white man out in front?"

Stupid Humans

BRENT SASS

Brent is a legend in mushing and was the first big name storyteller we ever had on the show. His story is encouraging to those of us who come to Alaska as adults and really aren't sure how you're supposed to do these Alaskan things, like hunting way out in the bush. His story shows you've got to start somewhere, so get out there and try to do it and hope none of the lessons you learn end up being lethal. He told this story at our November 2014 live event in Fairbanks.—Rob Prince

I came to Alaska fourteen years ago with one goal: to be an Alaskan. It took me a long time. The first four years I went to the university, and I didn't really enjoy that very much. I wanted to go out into the woods and do things in the wilderness, but I was kind of a city guy and didn't know how to do that sort of thing and didn't have anyone to show me. So I thought, "I'm just going to start doing this stuff." Then I had to find some buddies to do it with me. I got a couple guys together and we decided to go up north–way, way up north–and shoot some caribou. We really didn't have any idea what we were doing, but we were going to try it. These guys, Josh Horst and Matt Fraver, are two of my best friends now. I've since done hundreds of trips with Josh.

So we drove all the way up north on the haul road. We had a Scanoe, one of those flat-backed canoes, and more stuff than you can imagine. Our plan was park at Happy Valley and just motor up the Sagavanirktok River. Someone said it was a big river, but we figured we could make it in the Scanoe.

So we got there, put all our stuff in the Scanoe, and wondered, "Okay, where are *we* going to fit??" I guess we wanted to be prepared, and that's a good thing, but we were *really* prepared. We had the kitchen sink and we were going into the middle of the wilderness. I was used to camping out of the truck, so this was a transition for me, but we were learning. We got in, and I said, "We're just going to make it happen. Get on top of that stuff, Matt." So Matt was sitting on top of bags in the middle of this canoe and Josh was up in the front. He had a little hole to put his legs into so he could get kind of lower in the canoe.

We pushed out into the river and it turned out that yes, it *was* a big river. With the three of us and all our stuff in the canoe, we discovered we had about an inch of freeboard. In other words, the edges of the canoe were an inch above the surface of the water—maybe not quite an inch. And those guys were like, "Oh, God, what are we doing?! What are we doing, Brent?!"

I said, "Don't look at me! I'm not the leader here. We're doing this together. But I am going to make you do it. We're not turning around now. We just drove 300 miles up this road. Let's do it!"

I hit the gas on the five-horsepower motor. We were going up a huge river now . . . with a *five-horsepower motor*. We looked over at the bank. Basically, we were not moving forward. The current was too strong and we had way too much stuff. So those guys said again, "What are we doing?! What are we doing?!" They were anxiously bracing themselves against the sides of the canoe because if we tilted a tiny bit one way or the other, we were going into the river and then you would never hear from Brent, Josh, or Matt ever again.

So Plan B had to be developed real fast. We were not going to give up. We picked a spot on the other side of the river and motored over there. I slammed the boat up against the bank and floored the motor—I had to floor it just to keep from going back down the river. I yelled at those guys, "Get out, get out, get out!" So they jumped out with almost nothing. Josh had his gun and Matt had some bear spray, but that was it. Then I shoved back out. I said, "You guys just walk up the bank. We've only got two more miles to go." Our plan was to motor up the big river and then veer off onto a tributary and go another five miles up that. Then we'd shoot some caribou and come back down. I figured they could walk the two miles, I could handle the canoe, and we would be able to make much better speed. So I pushed back out into the river and we were all joyous. I was now making a little bit of progress. They were *walking* much faster than I was going, but we *were* making progress. I was excited. They were excited. We were doing it! We were out in the wilderness! It seemed to me there was not another soul for miles in any direction. I don't know—there may have been someone around the corner, but we felt like we were all alone in the middle of nowhere.

I looked up, just scanning the willows and the tundra and all of this beautiful, beautiful Alaska . . . and saw a *large* grizzly bear. It was about 100 yards away, up on this little plateau overlooking my buddies walking on the bank. So I yelled to my buddies, "Bear! Bear!"

Unfortunately they couldn't hear me very well and thought I was cheering them on, so they yelled back, "Yeah! Yeah! Let's do this!"

And I yelled back, "No! No! *Bear!*"

Finally they looked up. Suddenly they got very serious and shouted, "Oh! What are we going to do?!"

I said, "I don't know. Do you want to get back in the boat? Or do you want to take your chances with the grizzly bear?" The grizzly bear was a long way away at this point, so I decided, "Just deal with the grizzly bear, guys. We'll keep an eye on it."

But they didn't like that idea. "Get over here!"

So I motored over to the side and again slammed the boat into the bank, revving the engine as hard as I could because otherwise I was going to go away downriver again. To keep from floating away, I said, "Matt, grab the rope on the front of the boat."

He turned to grab the rope and I heard a *tsck* sound. He'd accidentally tapped the trigger of his bear spray. The wind was blowing toward me and a second later I got the spray full in the face. I hit the deck, coughing in the bottom of the boat. It was just a mild shot, not too bad, but for the moment I was blinded.

Josh was brandishing his gun wildly, shouting, "What are we going to do?!" and Matt was yelling, "I'm sorry, I'm sorry!" and I said, "I don't care. Where's the bear? How are we going to keep moving forward?"

I rubbed my eyes and when I could see again I noticed that the bear had moved twenty or thirty yards closer to us. I asked, "What do you guys want to do? Do you want to stay on the shore or get back in the boat?"

They said, "I think we should get in the boat."

"I don't think you should get in the boat," I said. "We're all three going to die if you get in the boat. We have a fighting chance against this grizzly bear."

They really thought they needed to get in the boat, but I insisted, "No. Just push me back out and I'll stay close to shore and we'll watch this grizzly bear." The whole time we were having this conversation the bear was getting closer and closer. It was probably about forty-five yards away, standing up, looking at us. We were still fighting against this raging river. We were yelling at each other. I know those guys pretty well now, but at this point I hadn't spent a second in the wilderness with these people and we didn't have a real good way to communicate. In the end I just said to Matt, "Push me out again! Use the paddle."

But Matt was still holding the bear spray. In the same motion of pushing me out, he sprayed a four-second squirt right into my face. I fell back into the bottom of the boat. Josh and Matt were on the bank asking, "Are you okay?!" Josh dropped his gun. The canoe started to float down into this little eddy. I was coughing. I could see nothing. My eyes were burning. We got the canoe off to the side of the bank and I said, "I need to get out of this boat. I can't see anything. Someone else needs to drive the boat if we're going to do this."

So I got out and for a time we all just sat there. Matt was scared I was going to clock him because he had just doused me *twice* with bear spray in a matter of about four minutes. But I said, "Don't worry about it, Matt. Where's that bear?" In all the excitement we'd actually forgotten about it for a bit. We looked up, and—this is God's honest truth—this bear, this very large bear, was standing on its hind legs about thirty-five yards away. I thought, "He could just come and eat us right now." But he looked at us, shook his head as if to say, "Stupid humans," dropped to all fours, and sauntered away.

I said, "Alright, well, I guess we survived the bear encounter, guys. Do you want to continue?" But the wind was out of our sails at that point, so we decided to pack it in and go home. We actually just pulled the canoe all the way back up the river. We didn't want to get into it anymore.

The moral of the story, however, is that you've got to start somewhere. You've got to take chances. You've got to go on adventures. That's what Alaska is for, and that's the reason I moved to Alaska. We talked about our experience the whole way home in the truck. We had made mistakes *before we left Fairbanks*, all the way up the haul road, with the canoe, with the bear (and one of us with the bear spray), but we had had the time of our lives and experienced the ingredients of a truly great adventure story.

"No," Matt said. "We can *never* tell this story, guys. We can never, *ever* tell this story."

And I said, "I'm telling this story to *everyone I know*, Matt— because it's the beginning of huge, epic adventures for all three of us."

I'm going to continue making these stories, and living in Alaska, and learning from Alaska.

My Jewish Mother

WENDY DEMERS

"Fish-out-of-water" stories are perennial favorites with audiences, and the story that Wendy Demers (pronounced "de-MESS") told is a wonderful and extreme example of that genre. Imagine going from New Jersey to a tiny, remote coastal village in Alaska that's accessible only by small airplane? If you can't imagine that, then she'll do it for you in this story she told at our first live show in April 2014.—Rob Prince

I remember it vividly. It was August 2, 2000, and I was on the smallest plane I had ever been on in my life. Ten seats, eight of which were taken up by young kids coming back to the village from church camp out in Nome, the pilot, and myself in the copilot seat. I don't know how I ended up so lucky . . . It was a clear day, but it was really windy, and I mean *windy*. In a small plane like that, you can feel just about everything.

We dropped off a few kids in a few villages. Then, as we were coming into Wales, the pilot told me, "You see those two islands out there? They're the Diomede Islands. The smaller one is American, and just a mile away there's Big Diomede—that's Russian. The international date line runs between them."

I said, "Oh, I didn't realize that on a clear day we actually *could* see Russia."

As we approached the village he said, "Well, we're just going to let everyone know we're arriving" because the airport in Wales,

Alaska, is just an airstrip. That's it. There are no buildings, just a runway. So we buzzed the village to alert everybody and then came in for a landing. I noticed as we were coming in that there were two broken planes, one on each side of the runway. "What happened?" I asked the pilot.

"Oh, there were a couple of inexperienced pilots who didn't know how the crosswinds work up in the peninsula. It's nothing to worry about. Nobody was seriously injured."

I asked, "You've been flying up here for a long time then?"

He said, "Oh, you know, a couple of months . . ." But we landed safely, I'm happy to say.

As the plane came to a stop, a bunch of people surged up to greet the kids. I was introduced to a gentleman named Eric, a teacher in the village, and a gentleman named Frank, the school's maintenance man. He'd brought with him his four-wheeler and a trailer to lug all of my stuff to the apartment I was going to be staying in. I had a couple of suitcases and an oversized fish box filled with halibut I'd caught in Valdez the week before.

He asked me, "What's in the box?"

"Oh, well, there's halibut," I said.

"*All of it?*"

"Well, there's a little bit of dry ice and some butter, but it's pretty much all halibut."

"Do you like to trade?" he asked.

"Well," I answered, "I knew I was coming to a reindeer herding village, and I was hoping that halibut would be good barter material, so yeah!"

He said, "Okay," then loaded everything onto the trailer. He hopped onto the four-wheeler and I hopped on the back.

On the way to my apartment I asked, "So, Frank, how far away from my apartment is the school?"

"Oh, about a quarter mile. In a couple of months it'll be half a mile." I thought he was just pulling my leg, but I'll get back to that . . .

Frank very kindly helped me take everything into my apartment. I'd been there maybe fifteen minutes when I heard a knock at my door. I opened it and there was Frank with a big smile on his face and the hind end of a reindeer on his shoulder. I'm talking belly, butt, legs, just up on his shoulder. "Where d'ya want it?"

I said, "The kitchen sink, I guess?" We decided how much halibut he was going to take and he left wearing an even bigger smile.

Ten minutes later I was still loading stuff into the freezer, wondering what I was going to do with all this deer in my sink, when there was another knock.

I opened the door to find a gentleman with long gray hair standing in the doorway. "My name's Clifford. I hear you have halibut for trade."

"Well, yeah, I do."

"I have some walrus," he offered.

"I'm a Jewish girl from Jersey," I said. "I have no idea what to do with walrus. Is it good?"

"Oh, it's real good. You'll love it!"

I shrugged. "Well, why not?"

So he traded me some walrus for some halibut and left with a big smile.

About fifteen minutes later there was another knock. It was the local pastor from the Lutheran church. He introduced himself, welcomed me to the community, and said, "I hear you have some halibut for trade."

"Yeah, I do," I said.

"I have some musk ox roast. Would you be interested?"

"Suuuure, why not?" So I traded him for some musk ox and he left with a smile and a "Thank you."

About ten minutes after that, there was yet *another* knock. I opened the door and a woman introduced herself. "My name's Lena. I'm an elder in the community and I'm inviting you for your first Eskimo dinner."

I said, "Great!"

"I live two doors that way," she said, pointing.

I said, "Alright, great!"

"I invited Eric to come too."

I said, "Super. What time is dinner? What time should I get there?"

"Dinner starts *when you get there*," she told me.

So I had been in town for about an hour, and already I'd met a handful of locals, including one of the teachers and the minister, and I had a freezer half full of halibut, musk ox, and walrus meat as well as the hind end of Rudolph in my sink. It was a pretty good first day.

The next morning, I called Jersey to let my folks know I'd arrived safely and everything was alright. I told my mother about the two-day trip out, the broken planes on the runway and, of course, having walrus my first night in town. And she said, in her stereotypical Jewish accent, "*Wendy, they don't have roads*? What do you mean they *don't have roads*? To get there, you couldn't drive? *And they have broken planes*? *They didn't get rid of the broken planes*? What's *wrong* with them? That's crazy! And oy vey! You ate walrus? Is it *kosher*?" She obviously didn't get it.

I found out about the middle of October that Frank hadn't been joking when he told me the distance from my apartment to the school would increase from a quarter mile to half a mile in a few months. The locals told me it wasn't safe to walk on the beach to school once winter set in because polar bears could come in on the ice flow. They said that as long as you're walking with someone slower than you, you're okay . . . but since I was alone, I figured I'd better walk through the community to get to school.

The wind in Wales is about twenty miles per hour, with lots of gusts. I've never seen or heard wind quite like it. It got to the point where I couldn't sleep when I came back to Fairbanks because it was too quiet. By the middle of October the snow started drifting. One morning I went to open my front door only to be faced with a wall of snow—there was only about a foot or two clear at the top of my door. I was really glad I'd left the shovel *inside*. I proceeded to use the shovel to make some holes in the snowdrift, pushed the shovel out the top of the door, and then followed it, sliding out like a seal on my belly.

Then came the work of digging out. After about thirty minutes, I had shoveled the snow down only to about thigh-high but I thought, "I'd better get going or I'm going to be late for school." On the way I saw the first huge snowdrift—it went all the way from one side of the path to the other. There was no getting around it. I knew the beach route wasn't an option because of the polar bears, so I had to walk through this snowdrift, which was about waist deep. I thought, "Well, it can't be too bad." I was wrong. The snowdrift was like quicksand. It took me a good ten minutes to wiggle all the way through it and I worked up a pretty good sweat. I realized that at this rate, with six or seven more drifts to cross through, I was going to be late for work. I looked around to see if there were any kids on their way to school because the local kids gave really good advice. Unfortunately there were none to be seen. I told myself sternly, "You're a teacher now; you should be able to figure this out." As I approached the next snowdrift, the light bulb went on—I realized I needed to disperse my weight. So I cinched my backpack tight, got down on all fours, and crawled up to the top of this drift. I started sinking as I got higher, so I quickly lay down and just barrel-rolled down the other side of it. It worked like a charm! I was pretty proud of myself. I was laughing and looking for somebody else to laugh with, but nobody was around. I proceeded to crawl and roll my way to school, all the while thinking, "I wonder if there are any other teachers in the world getting to school quite like this?"

The rest of the day proceeded pretty normally until about 3:00 in the afternoon when Lena came into my classroom, holding a grand-baby's hand with each of hers. She said, "Wendy, I was standing in my kitchen this morning looking out the window, sipping my coffee, and I saw you crawling and rolling. I turned to my husband and said, 'Raymond, *what in the world is that white woman doing?'*"

Needless to say, I was pretty embarrassed. I explained that I didn't think I was going to get to work any other way, and nobody was around to give any advice, so . . .

She looked at me and said, "We decided it's time to give you your real Eskimo name."

"Oh, that's great! What's my name going to be?" I asked.

"Anukli."

"What does that mean?"

She explained, "It means windy, like the wind outside. Now we can say, 'Anukli, it's anukli out!'"

Well, I heard that name a lot. It caught on very quickly.

During the Thanksgiving holiday they had a big potlatch at the school, and I really wanted to contribute. About a month before

Thanksgiving, I called my folks and asked my mom if she could send me a care package with some matzo ball soup mix and all the fixings. She did, and I got them in time—not at all a guaranteed thing. I made all the matzo balls at home the evening before and brought them to school quite early the next morning. Using one of the big pots in the kitchen I started cooking a huge pot of matzo ball soup.

When it was almost ready, Lina came into the kitchen, asking, "Whatcha cooking, Wendy?"

"You'll see; it'll be done soon." I said.

When it was finally done, I brought it out of the kitchen and set it on the table with all of the other food in the cafeteria. Lena was the first one to the pot. She took off the lid, grabbed the ladle, and started stirring. Scrunching up her eyebrows, she asked, "What's that floating in the soup?"

"Well, they're kind of like dumplings. They're called matzo balls. *You* fed me walrus my first night in town. Try it!"

Warily, she ladled a tiny amount—containing a single matzo ball—into a bowl. Everyone was watching her. She took one spoonful and her eyes lit up. Then she went right back and filled up her bowl. I'm proud to say that I fed 120 Eskimos matzo ball soup and I've got video footage to prove it. That was pretty cool.

My experience in Wales wasn't all fun and games, but I learned a lot about the Eskimo culture. I learned you can open up your jacket on a good windy day and it will act like a sail and just push you home. (The kids will tell you to make sure you lean into the wind or you could end up face-planting, which isn't pretty.) I learned that you don't need a good sled or a good pair of skis to enjoy the snowdrifts in town. You just need a good pair of slippery pants. I learned a lot about myself, too. I learned that you don't need a lot to be happy.

Rowdy

MIKE HOPPER

We have a lot of funny stories on Dark Winter Nights *because I love to laugh and I love to make people happy. But not all of life in Alaska is funny and happy and if our show is going to represent what life in Alaska is really like, we sometimes have to share the sad stories. We were deeply honored Mike was willing to share his difficult story of tragic loss with us just over a year after he experienced it. He shared this story live on stage at our April 2016 live event in Fairbanks.—Rob Prince*

I've told this story now about half-a-dozen times, and the audiences have always been other backcountry skiers and mountaineers. After losing my friend Eric Peterson and my dog Rowdy, I felt kind of a duty to share some of the things we learned, some of the mistakes we made. But I'm not going to talk to you about avalanches. I'll tell you what it's like to survive one, but I'm going to talk to you about a dog.

We got my dog Rowdy around the same time that we were scheduled to open our lodge in Black Rapids. It's in a beautiful place called Isabel Pass. I had waited a few years now to get a dog. The last dog I had was a red Siberian, and trying to keep him penned in at our home in Gold Stream Valley was a life's work. Trying to keep him penned in at our cabin in the Alaska Range turned out to be even more difficult. Now he runs with the wolves, as we say. So I was determined that before I got another dog I would wait until he could be with me all the time.

I picked Rowdy out of a litter of about ten puppies. I'll never forget: from the moment I put him in the front of my Dodge truck, he curled up next to me and promised never to go away. He was the dog every boy deserves. No matter how old the boy. I couldn't have trained him to do the things he did at our lodge, naturally and spontaneously. He would take people out for hikes in the woods and never come back without them. He had a way of begging for food that made *you* feel you'd received the gift when you gave him something.

But most of all, Rowdy loved to ski. I'm a backcountry skier, which is kind of like a hermit skier. You value the solitude of the mountains as much as your turns. Rowdy broke that solitude. I'm not the safest skier in the world. It goes against all avalanche protocol and safety concerns to ski alone, but Rowdy and I had a great time together. He wasn't even a year old when I first took him out in the mountains of Isabel Pass. Back then he was so small he would kind of disappear in the snow, but even then he would race me down the hill. He'd plunge up to his shoulders in snow, but he had big feet, and from day one I knew I had the right dog.

A few years ago it rained in mid-January. That was the first time I ever saw avalanches in Isabel Pass. They came down the next day like huge masses of porridge. They were just everywhere—I'd never seen anything like it. It destroyed our skiing for that year. So the following winter, 2014–2015, we were snow starved. We hadn't had any skiing to speak of the spring before. I was just chomping at the bit to go, as was Rowdy.

In December 2014 I got a text from my friend Eric Peterson: "Seven inches of fresh snow in Trim's Deep Camp. We're on." So he came rushing down from Delta Junction the next morning—a bright eyed, huge, muscular thirty-five-year-old guy, one of the most amazing mountaineers I've ever known—to join me and Rowdy.

It was December 6, so this really is a dark winter night's tale. The little sunlight there was pretty flat. We didn't care. We hadn't skied in over a year. So we started up this little pass, sort of a notch in Rainbow Ridge, a big sweeping ridge with a notch at the end of another peak. If you go up through that notch you reach some of the most easily accessible and beautiful skiing in the Isabel Pass area. We ski it all the time for our first runs of the season because the snow arrives early and you can get high real fast—I mean legally . . . As you approach the crest of this little notch it serves as a little pass into another drainage. There's a side valley that shoots off, and then you turn left up that valley to a side valley. As you go up this side valley, to your right are ridges of 1,500–2,000 vertical feet. There are these spines coming down creating all these side valleys. The cool part is you can go up and ski all those spines. There are three or four little valleys as you go up. The valley we were going up that day ends in a huge bowl. Skiers love this whole area because it offers so much choice—you can ski anywhere and experience anything, depending on your skill level and what the snow looks like. I'd done it many, many times.

I won't bore you with descriptions of the warning signs we noticed yet chose to ski past, but suffice it to say we were a little nervous going up. But we kept poking the snow to test its stability. The further up we got, the deeper the snow got, and the more solid it seemed to us.

As you get to the far end and reach this bowl, there's one last spine coming down, marking the end of this ridge and the beginning of the big bowl. You have to hug your way up around that far side of this spine coming down. We'd begun that final approach; coming up out of the valley floor to the top is about a half-mile final ski up. We had gone about two-thirds of the way up that final approach when it started to steepen. Just as it did that, my friend Eric, who was in front just as he always was, noticed something different about the snow. He drew my attention to it. Underneath this new six inches of fresh snow was a chunky layer of yellow hardened snow. We hadn't seen anything like that down lower and we both were pretty nervous at that point. As experienced backcountry skiers, we did not like the feel of it. That hardened layer is what snow can slide on. Any snow that falls on top of it at a certain angle is prone to sliding off as avalanches. We immediately started talking about hugging this spine because we noticed as you got to the snow on the spine, it was all good. We weren't unaware that we were in a dangerous situation, but we hoped to mitigate the danger by hugging this spine. We actually got to the point where we were making mental notes to ourselves of rocky outcroppings so we could stay off the dangerous section.

It wasn't four minutes after we'd noticed that change in the snow that we heard a distant *whumpf*. We could barely hear it, but we instinctively knew what it was. It's a sound you don't like to hear, the sound of a layer of snow that had been precariously perched on a fragile layer beneath it collapsing. If this collapse happens on a steep enough angled slope, that's how avalanches start.

Eric was about twenty feet ahead of me and Rowdy was right behind him. Gazing up the slope, I saw what looked like a twelve-inch white water wave about twenty-five feet from me. It is amazing how fast your mind works under these circumstances. I knew immediately what it was. I also knew I was toast. I felt unbelievably powerless. I still had skins on my skis. I was pointing uphill, sideways, to this wave coming at me. I couldn't outrun it. There was literally nothing I could do. I was going to be, and I knew it, a tree chopped down right at the ankles.

Yet I was still registering my chances—and Eric's and Rowdy's. As I turned back to see my friend and my dog, I thought Eric was safe. He was over closer to the spine and further uphill than I was. I thought he was out of the path of this avalanche. I saw Rowdy bolting for all he was worth to reach the safety of the spine. But already his hindquarters had been caught up in the wave. I knew Rowdy was engulfed. I knew I would be too, but I had an avalanche beacon on. I called out to Eric, "Watch for Rowdy!" I figured Eric would be able to track me down, but Rowdy didn't have a beacon on. I wanted to make sure he kept eyes on Rowdy so he could get him first, and then come for me. That was my thinking.

I don't remember being hit by the avalanche. It was what is called a soft snow avalanche. Since the snow was some of the first of the season, it hadn't been wind affected yet. It hadn't turned into a hard compact thing. It was soft snow, but a slab. The distant *whumpf* indicated that it had actually broken away from the existing snow far up on a ridge, 400–500 yards upslope from us. We'd walked right into it. Boom!

My next memory was of sliding on my stomach in total darkness, headfirst. Just sliding downhill moving super fast. I remember going through a checklist of all the things I'd learned in avalanche classes about what you're supposed to do if you get caught. The first thing is swim to the surface. Well, that was like trying to swim in white water, so it took me only a split second to realize that was a dumb idea. I wasn't going to get anywhere. There was no purchase. It was all black fluff around me. The next thing I remembered to do was one of the things that saved my life—keep the area in front of your face clear. As I helplessly slid, I frantically wiped my hands in front of my face to create a clear space. I also remembered that snow packs into any orifice, so I squeezed my eyes and shut my mouth as tight as I could.

The slide seemed to go on forever. I was conscious the entire time. I was going through calculations about how long this could last and where I was on the mountain. My only real fear was if it went too long, I would end up in the bowl at the bottom of the valley buried beyond recovery. It's called a terrain trap. You go down in the snow and it just keeps piling on top of you if you hit the bottom of the valley. So the only worry I had, and this is really kind of odd, was if it was going to stop or take me all the way to the bottom. If I got to the bottom, I knew I was dead. It was with a kind of quiet certainty that I accepted that fact, but I was certainly hoping to stop. And sure enough, slowly it stopped.

The minute it stopped, I shoved all the snow that I'd been keeping away from my face. I was completely confident that I would find air. When I look back now, I realize I had absolutely no reason to expect that—but at the time I was sure that if the slide stopped, I would be okay. I shoved the snow away from my face and there was air. I took a *huge* first breath. You're not aware when you're sliding like that that you're holding your breath. I had no awareness of that. There was never a panic about losing my breath or not having enough air. When I stopped, though, I ended up sucking in a huge mouthful of snow. I don't know how that happened because I had my mouth shut the whole time. I spit that out and noticed there was a lot of blood on it. I don't know where that came from. But then I was able to take a lungful of air and tried to assess my situation. I found that even though I just slid on my stomach the whole way down, I ended up propped upright slightly at an angle.

All I had cleared was my face and my right hand. Everything else was pinned. The snow was over my head but I had a kind of window out of which I could—theoretically—shovel snow. But it was like being trapped in sand. As I shoveled the snow out, it all started sliding back in on me. At that point I figured I couldn't get myself out, but I did have a ski pole on the wrist of my free right hand. I took it off, reached up with it as far as I could, and stuck it out of the snow. I was convinced Eric was still free, although I didn't know about Rowdy. I tried yelling once but sound doesn't carry real well when you're buried in the snow. I waited a couple minutes until it started to dawn on me that if anyone was going to do any rescuing, it might have to be me. I found that if I used the little basket on the end of the ski pole, I could shove small spoonfuls of snow out of the hole. Gradually I began to realize that I had ended up near the leading edge of the avalanche, which allowed me to push the snow out. If I'd have been back a foot further, I couldn't have done what I did. You have to have someplace to push the snow; you can't just push it straight up.

Over the next couple hours I was able to shove big tablespoons of snow away as I dug with my right hand. Slowly, slowly, slowly, I was able to dig enough away to enable me to reverse the ski pole and chop myself out, free my upper body, reach behind, and grab a snow shovel. By that point I knew I was good. I dug myself out. I did manage to wrench my knee in the process because I started getting cramps. That's how long it took. I tried to pull my feet out of my ski boot, and that didn't work. But I finally was able to dig down to my feet, discovering then that I still had my skis on, which was another thing that saved me. I bent down, unclipped my skis, and crawled out of my hole. I put on every item of clothing I had with me as a precaution against hypothermia and went to look for my avalanche beacon. I struggled to turn it to "receive" so I could use it to track the signal of Eric's beacon. I looked uphill; about twenty feet away from me I saw something black in the snow. I scrambled over to it. It was Eric's ski glove. He had done what I had—try to reach the surface. He had *just* reached it.

I dug down to him, but I . . . I sort of knew he was gone. It had been two and a half hours since the avalanche by that point. I didn't have much experience with death but there's a life force in people—when it leaves them, there's no question they're gone. I regret now that I didn't feel for a pulse, but there wasn't any doubt in my mind. Now I had to concentrate on getting myself out before I froze to death. I looked very briefly for Rowdy, but I knew I wouldn't find him.

I went back to where I had been trapped, dug my skis out, and put them on. It was dark by then, but I had a headlamp. We had started our trip at about 10:30 a.m., the avalanche was around 1:30 p.m., and it was probably around 4:30 p.m. by the time I skied back toward the highway. I don't remember much of the ski out. Then I had to wait by the side of the road for hours before I could get a ride. The key to the truck was with Eric. I ended up at the emergency room.

The troopers called in an avalanche expert from Valdez. At my advice they didn't conduct an immediate search the night of the avalanche. I warned them off because I knew it was dangerous to go up there. The troopers cordoned off the whole area, telling no one to go in. They told me it would be summer or spring before they could attempt a recovery, which wasn't what I wanted to hear.

So on December 21, the true middle of winter, a buddy of mine, who was on his honeymoon at the lodge, and I decided to go up to see what the conditions looked like. We scared ourselves getting there, but we found the spot where Eric was buried. I had marked it with an avalanche probe. We discovered at that time the true extent of the avalanche. It wasn't just one avalanche that broke up above us at that side of the spine. It also broke off in the adjoining valley. It was basically two huge avalanches that had come together. The fact that our avalanche beat the other one down the slope was the reason I survived. If the other slide had come down first and we hit the side of it, I wouldn't have made it either. So, really, I shouldn't be here today for a number of reasons.

We dug down to find Eric. You could tell from the position of his body that—true to his nature—he had fought the whole way down. I knew when I saw the avalanche and then was knocked over that it was useless to fight, but he was bigger, stronger, and more aggressive than I was. He fought the whole way down.

If there's any grace in this story, it's that when we got Eric's upper body uncovered, we found Rowdy, curled up against Eric's back. In front of his face was an iced-over cave. If I'd been completely buried and couldn't move the snow out of that hole, I might have been able to keep a cave in front of my face. The problem is as you exhale, it coats that cave with ice, until you can't pull the oxygen from the snow any longer and you slowly, slowly go to sleep and die. Well, my friend Rowdy, curled up against Eric's back, dug a cave with his front feet. From the expression on his face and his position, I could tell that he'd just gone to sleep. His right paw was on Eric's shoulder.

We brought them both down. It took us two days.

In a sense Rowdy never left those mountains. I believe that when someone's caught in an avalanche he's still there, providing some comfort to people in their last minutes of life. It's the only solace I can take from this.

Kidnapped

ROY CHURCHWELL

It can be a tough trip moving up to Alaska, but Roy certainly takes the cake for strangest ways to get here that I've ever heard. Like Alexandra Dunlap, he was selected as an audience storyteller, so none of us had any idea what was coming when he started his story. After you read it, you'll understand what was going through our minds at the time. He shared this story at one of our small live events in January 2016.–Rob Prince

This is a story of how I first came to Alaska, but it doesn't start in Alaska. I was born in Arizona. My parents had split up by the time I was born, partly because of my mother's addiction to drugs.

As a result of her addiction, I started out in life as a bit of a criminal. At four years old I helped my mom finance her drug habit by breaking into houses. She'd boost me through a window and I'd walk around to unlock the back door for her. She'd sell what she stole to pawn shops and spend the money on drugs.

My dad desperately wanted to get me out of this situation, but the courts wouldn't let him–he had no proof that this activity was going on. So he indulged in his own bit of lawbreaking: kidnap. One day when my mother had dropped my little brother and me off at my dad's mother's house, he and my stepmom simply picked us up and headed for Alaska.

It was 1979. I was only about four, but I still remember quite a few things about that amazing trip. We drove through Canada in a truck pulling an Airstream trailer. We did a lot of camping. I remember stopping at one place that was owned by the First Nations where I met a young kid who had this awesome talking raven perched on his shoulder. To this day I want a raven that sits on my shoulder. I remember looking down into a lake from a dock one day and seeing what I thought was a huge alligator. I went running back to tell my dad, who told me it was a pike waiting under the dock for prey to pass by. I'm pretty sure that fish was as big as I was.

It was a little hairy for my dad and my stepmom at the Alaska-Canada border. There was a good chance, my dad thought, that the border patrol might ask him some difficult questions about these kids coming through. I guess he must have looked Alaskan enough because they let him through.

We drove to the first town, Tok, and set up in a Bureau of Land Management campground outside of town. At that time, you could basically camp for as long as you wanted in one place, and we did that. My dad was hoping to get a full-time job and make a life for us in Alaska. My stepmom really wanted a cabin, and in those days if you couldn't get a cabin, you would build a wannigan. Which my stepmom says was slang for "If you want a cabin but you can't afford one, you build a want-a-gan." So we built a wannigan in the BLM campground. It's basically a three-walled log structure that you support against, in this case, the Airstream trailer. We lived in there for most of the fall. We ate a lot of squirrels, grouse, and snowshoe hares. We were pretty poor at that time.

My brother and I didn't get spanked very often, but when you get spanked, it's pretty memorable. Parents were allowed to spank in those days. My stepmom always made these English muffins with raisins in them, and I decided that they kind of looked like boogers. I commented on this for such an extended period that my dad finally decided that that was enough and told me to quit it. But as kids sometimes do, I took the joke one step too far and said, "Mmm, boogers . . ." So I got a spanking for that.

The other spanking I remember was one I actually didn't get—my little brother did. On a camping trip out to Eagle, my parents were in the tent and my brother and I were sleeping in the back of the truck. For some reason my brother decided to take off—he was just gone in the morning. My dad tracked him down to the Yukon River. He was very upset, pretty sure my brother had drowned. Not quite ready to give up yet, he looked around town. On the main street of Eagle he saw our yellow lab, Buster, sitting outside a bar. My dad went inside to discover my brother on a barstool eating French fries that some guy had given him. My little brother got a few spankings on the way home that day.

My dad did a lot of hunting but he was technically breaking the law by doing so without a license. Actually bothering to get a hunting license was not that common in Alaska in 1979, but he decided to be an upstanding citizen and do it anyway. At that time, when you applied for a hunting license they ran your name to see if you had any prior convictions. When they did that they found out my dad had kidnapped us and was wanted in Arizona.

Interestingly, although they could have just apprehended him right there and flown him down to Arizona, they didn't. That would have left my stepmom and us two kids in an illegal wannigan on the outskirts of a BLM campground outside of Tok. So they said he could take us himself back down to Arizona as long as we left right away. So we gave the wannigan to friends so that they could cut it up for firewood. I think they used the plywood and the stove to make a sauna.

When we got back down to Arizona, my brother and I stayed with our biological mom for a little while, but she decided that having two kids around was a little more work than she was interested in doing. It was only a couple of weeks or a month before, thankfully, we were back living with my dad.

That was an amazing summer and one that I still remember fondly. It was one of the reasons I decided to come back to Alaska to go to graduate school.

The Birthday Present

KAT BETTERS

*Kat's story is one that, honestly, I still can't figure out to this day.
It boggles the mind, but in a good way where something wonderful
happened—just in a very inelegant way. She shared this story live
on stage at our November 2015 live event in Fairbanks.
—Rob Prince*

My story takes place in the summertime about five or six years ago
when I was driving home up and over Ballaine Hill in Fairbanks. As
I was descending into the Goldstream Valley, I saw something little
and brown lying in the middle of the road. My first thought was
that it was a squirrel, but as I got closer I realized that it was an
ermine. Also called short-tailed weasels, ermines are in the weasel
family. They are about seven to ten inches long, very slender, and
look like they could probably run through a paper towel tube. Their
legs are situated way, way back in their caboose and their front
legs are way up front, so that when they run, they lope along like
a slinky. They are white in the winter with a little black tail, and in
the summer they are brown with a white underbody.

Ermines are not particularly uncommon or endangered, but they
are pretty elusive and it's rare to see one. That made it really dis-
heartening to see it lying in the road, especially since they are terribly, terribly cute, so cute it hurts.

At this time I was dating a man who worked at Fish and Game in the education and outreach department. Mike is a biologist and a naturalist and a tracker. The next day happened to be his birthday, so I was like, "Woo-hoo! There's an ermine lying in the middle of the road! Early birthday present! #1 girlfriend!" You probably think this is quite weird, which it is, but if you know Mike you know this is something he would actually be really, really excited about.

So I decided I was going to get him that ermine. I pulled over on the side of the road and popped the trunk to get a Ziploc bag (because when you date a biologist, you have things in your car like Ziploc bags and latex gloves because you never know when you're going to find something interesting on the side of the road—case in point). While I was doing this, another car stopped directly across the road from me. Gasp! My first thought was "He wants my ermine!" . . . as if any rational human being would want to scoop up roadkill. However, since that was exactly what *I* was doing, it got my hackles up and I started walking very quickly out into the road to establish my claim over that ermine.

A big, burly dude got out of the car and yelled over to me, "Do you know what that is lying in the middle of the road?" He looked really distraught, actually on the verge of tears. I said, "Yeah it's an ermine," and he said, "I have never seen one before. I am the one who hit it. I feel terrible. Do you think there is any way we could take it to the veterinary clinic at the top of Ballaine Hill?" At that point I was actually *holding* the ermine in my hand. If this thing was going to be okay, *I wouldn't be holding it.* Also, it was flopped over my hand like a wet noodle, there was blood coming out of its nose, and even though I could feel a faint heartbeat, this thing was a goner. I told him as much and I said, "Hey, but it's going to get a second life in the education outreach department at Fish and Game. It will get taxidermied and put into their collection so people can learn about ermines and how cute they are." He didn't seem at all happy about this outcome, but he got into his car and drove away. I put the ermine in the Ziploc bag, zipped it up nice and tight, and placed it in a box in the trunk so it wouldn't slide all around. I closed the trunk and drove home.

I had been home for about half an hour when I realized there was something I'd forgotten to do in town. So back into town I went, thinking, "Oh, I'll swing by Fish and Game and drop off Mike's birthday present early. Oh, won't he be excited!"

When I got to Fish and Game Mike wasn't there, but lot of other people I know were, so I spent the next half hour talking to everybody. Finally someone said, "Oh, hey, I just saw Mike out in the parking lot." Perfect—that was where he needed to be because that was where the ermine was. So I ran out there and called him over: "Sweetie, I've got something for you. It's an early birthday present!" He came over and I added, ". . . but you have to close your eyes." He dutifully closed them. I popped the trunk to get the dead ermine out . . . instead I pulled out a *very alive and pissed off* ermine. This poor, adorable little critter had steamed up the inside of the Ziploc bag. It had pooped in there, it had peed in there, and it was frantically trying to claw its way out.

I felt horrible. First of all, I couldn't believe what I was seeing—that it was *alive*. Second, I couldn't bear to see it trapped in there a second longer. I am not a screamer, but at that moment I was screaming as I ran to let it out of the bag at Creamer's Field. Mike opened his eyes to see my hind end running to the field dangling something while screaming so loudly that a crowd started to gather. Four or five other workers all came running over. Mike caught up to me as I got to the edge of the field and immediately recognized that in my bag was a hermetically sealed little ermine. Just as I was about to open it he yelled, "Stop! No! You can't open it here! It's not its natural habitat." Yeah, habitat, schna-bitat. I was still freaking out as I proceeded to explain to him that we were *not* walking another ten minutes to get this thing to its habitat down by the pond in the woods. Mike very quickly realized there was no reasoning with me, so we let it go right there.

I remember there was this moment of palpable silence as everyone stood watching. We knelt down and spun the bag around so the head of the ermine would come out of the opening. As we let it out I was expecting it to run out into fresh air and freedom. That's not what happened. It turned right back around, into the bag, and tried to claw its way out. So we spun the bag back around and I thought, "Okay, this time it'll go out." Nope, was not having it. It ran straight back into the bag again, continuing to try to claw its way out. Finally we realized, "You know, I think we can outwit this thing. It only weighs about a pound and a half." So we just shook it out, and there went Mike's birthday present, slinkying full speed across the field. I swear to you that it stopped for a moment, looked at us, scowled (mostly at me), put its feet down, and just ran, never to be seen again.

We were all left just standing there, absorbing the absurdity of what had just happened. Mike finally broke the silence: "So, Kat, how did you go about getting a live ermine into a Ziploc bag?" A valid question. I explained everything that had happened. Mike summed up: "So, let me see if I've got this right . . . It got hit by a car, put into a Ziploc, into a box, into a trunk, driven around for an hour, and when it finally came to, it was ten miles away from where it started its day." I admitted, "Yeah, that pretty much sums it up." A moment passed. Then he said, "You know, I could have you cited and ticketed for transporting wildlife without a permit." I said, "Yeah, honey, you do that."

Moose Mountain Celebrity Yard Farming Cooperative

BILL SCHNABEL

Many stories on Dark Winter Nights involve people goofing things up. When people ask me how best to tell a story about a goof up they made that they are really not proud of, I direct them to this story Bill Schnabel told on stage at our November 2014 live show in Fairbanks. He shows it's possible to tell a story about a mistake you made in a way that doesn't diminish the seriousness of the mistake and shows you really do regret how those events occurred.—Rob Prince

A few years ago, our neighbor Cathy said, "You know, I think this year we're going to raise chickens. We're going to feed the neighborhood."

Not to be outdone, I responded, "Oh, yeah, Cathy? Well, we're going to raise hogs!"

One of the great things about Fairbanks is the can-do spirit of its residents. If you want to mush dogs, all you need to do is work for a dog musher for a little while, get yourself a dog team, and pretty soon you're running the Iditarod. If you want to climb mountains, you drive south, or you drive north—and there are ranges in both directions you can climb. If you want to build a house, you go to Spenard's, get yourself some lumber, start hammering it together, and see what comes up. And if you want to raise hogs, you slap together a fence in your backyard, make some phone calls, and you're a hog farmer. That is exactly what we did. Over the course of that spring we read books and watched YouTube to learn how to raise hogs. I asked my friends Luke and Emily if they would help me build a hog pen, and they did. We got an electric fence and strung it around some trees. Then we built a house out of plywood and metal we had sitting in the garage. Finally, I built a trough out of lumber and we were ready to go.

I called a guy named Jerry in North Pole whom I had heard had hogs. He had gotten a truckload of hogs that he had diverted from a life in a confined feeding operation in Canada and brought here to North Pole. I went over to Jerry's house in early May, picked up three little forty-pound hogs about eight weeks old—little pink jobbies—and put them in a dog kennel in the back of my truck. They all fit into a single dog kennel at that point.

I won't go into too many details about what we learned that summer. I can summarize that information in just a few simple rules:

> RULE #1: Do not give your hogs clever names because then
> it will be difficult to kill them (or arrange to have them
> killed) at the end of the summer. We named our hogs My
> Hammy, Ham I Am, and Francis Bacon.
>
> RULE #2: Do not grow attached to your hogs for the same
> reason as in rule #1. My Hammy was the timid one. He
> would kind of back away from us fearfully; you'd have
> to entice him over with some food. Ham I Am was the
> friendly one. She would come up to you and rub her
> flanks against your leg, asking you to scratch her belly
> and behind her ears. Francis Bacon was the aggressive
> one. She was evil inside, she was. She would come up and
> headbutt you as you were trying to walk over to feed her,
> tripping you. If our hogs were the Three Stooges, Francis
> Bacon would have been Mo—the bossy one no one likes as
> much as the others. Despite all of that, we loved them. We
> absolutely loved our hogs.
>
> RULE #3: Do not expect your children to embrace the hog
> farming lifestyle that you and your wife have embraced. Our

children turned out to be embarrassed by hogs. They did not want their friends to know that we had hogs, and when we said, "Children, go out and slop the hogs," like they do on *Little House on the Prairie*, they said, "No! We will not do this!" In fact, every morning my wife Cheryl would feed the hogs and every afternoon I would feed the hogs.

RULE #4: Be careful what you feed your hogs. If you feed your hogs dry crushed barley, the dry crushed barley *going into* the hog looks exactly like the dry crushed barley *coming out* of the hog. You have to soak it overnight. It has something to do with enzymes being activated. Also, do not overfeed your hogs. The prime slaughter weight for a hog of this variety is 200 to 220 pounds. We surpassed that weight in early August and slaughtered them in mid-September. Our biggest hog was *317 pounds*, half again as large as it should have been. This not only makes it difficult to maneuver the hog . . . it also makes it hard to kill.

As summer waned, the rains came, and the leaves turned yellow, it became time to think about slaughtering the hogs. I asked my next-door neighbor Kate, who is always ready for the zombie apocalypse and knows something about guns, "Kate, do you have a gun?" She said, "Yes. I have a .38 Special." I thought to myself, "Hmmm .38 Special . . . My only experience is the band .38 Special, whose concert I saw in the mid-1980s." So I said, "Kate, will you slaughter my hogs?" and she said, "No, I cannot. I have grown too attached to them." Well, I certainly couldn't slaughter the hogs because I loved the hogs. So I asked my friend Luke. I said, "Luke, will you slaughter the hogs?" and he said, "Well, Emily and I have been giving you slop to give to the hogs all summer, so no, I don't feel comfortable killing them. But I have a buddy named Bjax from Wisconsin who is a hunter and has killed lots of stuff." We asked Bjax, the Wisconsin hunter, to shoot the hogs and he said yes.

September 16 was the allotted date when we were going to slaughter the hogs. It was a fall day, pretty outside, yellow leaves, fifty degrees. It was a Thursday afternoon. We agreed to meet at our house at 5:00 p.m. after work. Everybody showed up. My wife

Cheryl decided she and the kids were not going to attend. They had loved the hogs too much. But Cheryl did stop over at Fred Meyer's to get a berry pie off the discount rack that she thought might be useful to us.

In attendance that afternoon was me, Kate from next door, Luke, Bjax, and Emily. First we made a plan for how we would perform our mission and took our places. Then Luke and Kate and I opened the door to the hog pen. I had the pie. I called, "Come on out." Francis Bacon came out first because she was the most assertive. We closed the door after her because we didn't want the first two to see what happened to this one. We all walked across the yard, Luke on one side of Francis Bacon and Kate flanking her on the other side so she wouldn't get away. We walked by the house, over the driveway, and then down a little hill until we were under the tree house. I looked around at my fellow humans and we all made meaningful eye contact. I set the pie on the ground.

Now, when a hog eats dry crushed barley, they move their head around a bit. We had planned for this—I had told Bjax she might move her head a little. However, when a hog eats a virgin berry pie, a delicacy it has never eaten before, it moves its head around *a lot more*. I noticed this and I thought, "Well, this is a problem, but it's not my problem because I'm not shooting the hog." So I turned to Bjax and said, "Bjax, it's time." And I stepped away.

Bjax stepped up to her, planted the .38 Special between her eyes as best he could, and pulled the trigger. Boom! What I expected to happen was that the hog would fall flat down on the ground, kick a little bit, and I would cut her throat to bleed her out. But she had a really thick bony part of her head because of her 317 pounds, so when that gun went off she did not die. She looked directly at Bjax, because he had shot her. Then she looked directly at me, because I had loved her.

Then she turned around and walked away to the middle of the yard. I said, "Bjax, shoot her again!" By this time she was turning in circles, so Bjax was swinging his arm around trying to aim at her. He shot her again in the head, but she still did not die. She kept circling. I shouted, "For God's sakes, Bjax, shoot her again!" and he shot a third time. She was moving so much at this point that I do not believe he shot her in the head. He might have shot her in the foot. I'm not sure, but he did hit her because she sat down on her haunches and screamed the loudest hog screech I have ever heard in my life. It rattled the windows. It started the dogs down the street howling. It turned my knees to jelly. About that time our friend Bob, who was late for the event, showed up and got out of his car. He heard the gunfire and dove behind the door for fear of ricocheting bullets. Those three bullets didn't put her down. Francis Bacon ran up the hill and began thrashing against the side of my truck where Emily was sitting watching over things. I said, heart trembling, "Bjax, for God's sakes, go shoot her again!" so he ran up to her and shot her behind the ear and she finally dropped. I walked slowly up the hill and waited for her to stop kicking. Then I bent down to cut her throat. As I did so, with the last ounce of her life force she gave one final kick with her back leg; later I found a bruise on my shin in the shape of Iowa about the size of a softball. I cut her throat while I lay on the ground, writhing in pain. I watched the lifeblood flow out of her.

I looked at Francis Bacon. I looked at Emily in the truck with blood spattered on her shirt. I looked at Luke and Kate standing there trembling. I looked at Bjax, mortified, a tear in his eye and smoke coming out of the barrel of that .38 Special, and it occurred to me that life is tenacious. Life wants to hang on, and like every good farmer and every good hunter knows, if you are going to take a life, you'd better respect that life. You'd better cherish it.

Bjax was able to dispatch the other two hogs that night without incident by shooting them behind the ears. In subsequent years I and other members of the Moose Mountain Celebrity Yard Farming Cooperative have humanely dispatched many other hogs. But that first night . . . that first one . . . Francis Bacon—we gave her a bad death. I will always be ashamed of that. We did save her from life at a confined feedlot operation and for four and a half months we raised her in our backyard and gave her a damn good life. And we loved her. Man, that's gotta count for something.

Kneepads

CHRIS ZWOLINSKI

When people ask me to give them an example of the kind of stories I'm looking for for Dark Winter Nights, I always bring up this story from Chris Zwolinski. It has what I call "layers of weirdness." One thing goes wrong and then another thing on top of that and so on and so forth until the situation quickly snowballs. We all have stories about times one thing went wrong, but it's the stories where lots and lots of things went wrong, one after another, that I select for Dark Winter Nights. He told this story on stage at our November 2015 live event in Fairbanks and went on to become an invaluable part of our executive producer team.–Rob Prince

There were three of us. Mark and Eldon, who are brothers, and myself. Not one of us had any whitewater rafting experience. I mean, it's something we always wanted to do. We'd watched it on TV, read about it in the magazines. The brochure looked good. But it didn't involve us. We just wanted to do it.

It was 1985. I hadn't been up here very long, but just being in Alaska was a thrill for me. It still is. I would get out hiking and bicycling whenever I could, but the only rafting that we did was floating on the Chena River through town. And the only whitewater we'd see is if a power boat went by too fast next to us. We had one of those blue and yellow vinyl rafts that we bought at Pay & Save and we would blow it up and put in at Pioneer Park in Fairbanks, float past all the houses with nice trim lawns, and end up at Pike's Landing restaurant. That was the extent of our river experience.

Until one day when Eldon bought a new raft. At a garage sale. It was about 10 feet long and made of yellow rubberized canvas. It was a six-man raft, and I know this because it said so in big block letters along each side: SIX MAN RAFT. And it had something like a thin clothesline rope attached to the outside of it for carrying or towing it, or I don't know what. We weren't rafters.

Mark and Eldon had been down to Chitina fishing that week during heavy rains. On their way home they were paying close attention to the Delta River where it parallels the road and took notice of how fast the water was moving. When they arrived back in Fairbanks, they informed me that we were going whitewater rafting on the Delta River, to which I replied, "That's great! Let's go! I'm in! Where's the Delta?" I'm not so sure how or why that new raft gave us any new rafting capabilities, but nonetheless we threw the boat and our gear into the truck and drove south.

It's a three-hour drive from Fairbanks to the first point where we can clearly see the Delta River. This is where the Black Rapids River pours into the Delta. There is a big pull off on the highway there. We got out of the truck, and they presented this river to me and I go, "Whoa . . ." The water is just boiling and my enthusiasm about all of this is waning a little bit. I'm getting skeptical, but they assured me, "No, this is where we're going to take out of the water." But even looking upriver, the water is just rolling as it spills over the rocks. I look at them and say, "Are you sure?" I distinctly remember the comment back to me was, "Ahh! It will be fine! If anything goes wrong, we'll just paddle to shore, hike to the road, and hitch a ride back to the truck." So I thought, "Well. Okay. That's . . . that's an escape route." So we jump back in the truck and drove about 20 miles upriver on the highway.

I've done a little research since then and I've learned that the point where we stopped to go into the river is where the guidebook says that inexperienced rafters. . . . that would be us, generally get out after rafting the upper stretch, which is more placid. Uninformed of this important little detail, we pump up our boat, haul it into the river, and put on our life jackets. We took some extra clothes with us in a not-so-waterproof bag, and some snacks. That was it.

We get into the water, and at this point the river is pretty braided. It's so shallow that we end up walking a little bit, towing the raft, jumping back in, floating for a while, and then getting out and towing the raft some more. That went on for about an hour, but it was okay. It was a gorgeous, sunny day. There was a beautiful, blue sky and we were in the middle of the mountains. This was fantastic! We proceed like this until the river channels up and we find ourselves floating down more consistently.

Another hour passes, and the current is getting a little faster. There are a lot of glacial creeks coming in, the water is turning grey, and it's definitely getting colder.

Okay. I don't know who did it first, but one of us took off their life jacket and put it underneath their knees to insulate against the cold floor of the raft. The other two of us followed suit, and thought, "That's a good idea! It's much more comfortable this way. Besides, we're going to put the life preservers back on when we need them. I mean, that only makes sense!"

Again, it's a gorgeous day in the mountains, we're just loving it, and about an hour later, we see our first standing wave. This is going to be exciting! We paddle straight toward it, line up, and hit that wave straight on and just float right over the top. It was so anticlimactic. But not to worry! There was another one to the left! So we paddled over to that one and we hit it straight on as well, and just kind of float over it again. But we were enjoying it, chasing these waves. We were like a pin-ball paddling to the left or right! Some of them were a little stronger than others, but everything was going well. We thought we were gaining some experience and for the next hour, at least we were getting more confident at this as we chased the thrill.

Eventually the river starts tightening up and we don't have to paddle to the left and right so much to catch the waves anymore. The river is pretty much taking us where it wants to take us right down the center. We're going from roller to roller and the water is splashing and we're getting our money's worth here. This is . . . this is good. Then we hit a series of waves that was a little more than we had bargained for. There was a drop at the end of the row and the raft went in and flipped end for end upside down and tossed us into the water. When I came up, I was underneath the raft. I went back down and came back up outside of the raft and grabbed ahold of that clothesline running around the outside of the raft as Eldon and Mark were. The hydraulic was kind of keeping us in place and, if we had had any experience, maybe . . . maybe we could have held the raft there, flipped it, and climbed back in. But we have no experience. Our instincts said, "Get out of there! This is dangerous!" So we pushed off and immediately got sucked down under the next wave.

We're holding on and as we come out from under the water, we're spitting and coughing and quickly we learned to look ahead and scout. Sequence after sequence: When we approached the waves, we take a breath of air before the hydraulic would pull us down, which it did every single time. This got to be a regular thing, just seeing the wave, getting sucked underneath, popping back up, spitting and coughing up water. This went on for what seemed like a couple of minutes.

Then the water flattened out. It's still moving fast, but we can see a gravel bar off to the right. We start stroking and kicking with everything we had toward that gravel bar hoping we could make it. And we did! We touched ground! I had my feet firmly in the gravel. Mark got his feet in the gravel too. But Eldon's feet are tangled up in the rope coming off of the bow of the raft. (I didn't even know it had a bow). His legs were wrapped up and he had no control. He can't get his feet into the gravel. I'm holding on. Mark is holding on. We're both pulling with everything we have. I was almost up to my waist out of the water. Looking back, I guess I could have let go and been safe. But the thought never occurred to me. It never crossed my mind to just get out of the water and save myself. I just kept holding on with all my might, but the pull of the raft and Eldon sucked Mark and me back out and we were into the channel again, back into that routine, which we knew well: get a breath of air, get sucked down underwater in the rapids, pop back up, cough, and get ready for the next wave.

A couple more waves later I realized that I still had a paddle in my hand. Up to that point, I wasn't aware. Mark had a paddle in his hand, too. Eldon doesn't. But as soon as I realize I've got it, we hit another particularly violent wave and it pulled us down hard, ripping the paddle out of my hand.

This time, when I came back up, Mark wasn't there. I looked at Eldon and he's looking for his brother and he's not there and we don't know what to think. Then we locked eyes. For me, that exact moment while staring at Eldon was the most surreal and defining feeling of helplessness.

We looked at each other for a while. We are holding on. We didn't know what to say. We hit another hydraulic and it took us down again. When we came back up, we heard a voice. It was Mark. We didn't see him because he had worked himself around to the opposite side of the raft. What we didn't know was that he had a plan. He took his paddle and swung it over the upside-down raft and yelled at his brother to grab hold of it. At this point we were getting pretty numb and don't have a whole lot of grip strength. Eldon tried, and it took a couple of attempts, but he did finally manage to hold onto the paddle for a while. While he was doing that, Mark used the other end as a handle to pull himself up on top of the bottom of our boat. Then he hauled his brother up and then they hauled me on top.

So we're pretty excited here. We aren't exactly high fiving, but we think that maybe now we're going to make it. We start paddling with our arms and our one paddle when the current shoves us over to the right where there is a rocky cliff. We bounced off the wall, and then back into the channel, then we realized, quite dumbfounded, that we're sinking! One of the sharp rocks on that bank had sliced a hole into the raft. I'm kind of learning as we go here: I didn't know prior to that moment that the raft only had two chambers, a left and a right. I don't know which one was still holding air, but now the three of us are riding a yellow sausage! And we're on this thing. We are riding this thing.

Up ahead we could see the Black Rapids River and we don't think we can make it through what the water has in store for us after the junction of the two. Not riding a sausage. The river is about to get much more potentially fatal. We're paddling. We are trying to hold on to the sausage with one hand and paddle with the other. I happened to be in front, so Mark gave me the paddle, hoping I could steer it better. We don't know if we're going to make it to shore in time, so I yell at Mark to hold on to me. I'm going to let go of the raft and just furiously paddle using both hands on the handle. He told me later that with every stroke I made, the front of the sausage would come up in the air and go back down and come up in the air and bounce back down again. There was an eddy we were trying to aim for and the three of us work as hard as we possibly could to hit our target. And we didn't make it. Then it was like there was a countdown before the rivers joined and our fate was sealed: 150 feet . . . 100 feet . . . 75 feet . . . At about 15 feet before those rivers joined, my paddle hit solid ground. I jumped off, grabbed a rock, held the front of the sausage, and it pivoted around like a weathervane. Mark jumped out and was able to grab his brother and we dragged ourselves up on the shore—which was an incredible relief, and we could almost say we were safe. Except now we were on the wrong shore.

We were on the shore on the opposite side of the highway. We were literally right across the river from that pull off where we first inspected the water. Behind us was hundreds of miles of wilderness. Across from us was rescue and safety, and in between was this killer river.

At that pull off, there happened to be a young couple. Now, in my imagination, this guy has got his heartthrob out for a Sunday drive, and they stopped beside the road to look at the river, admire the Black Rapids Glacier in the mountains, and then they look upriver and say, "Whoa!! What's that?!" There they see this yellow sausage bobbing down the river with three guys on it, which is us, and they've probably never seen anybody rafting that way before. And hopefully they never see anything like it again.

After they watched us drag up onto shore, we tried to yell back and forth to them over the roar of the river. We were able to communicate that we are okay, but could they go about a mile or two up the road to the military Black Rapids Mountain Training Center for some possible help.

They did this, returning within 10 minutes. Over the noise of the water, we understood that help was coming, but the only word we heard was "hours." And they were right.

It was about three hours when three soldiers showed in an attempt to rescue us. What they had with them was a raft about half the size of ours and a fishing rod. They were yelling, trying to communicate, but it was like watching two mimes moving their arms and hands across the river from each other trying to give an idea of what's going to happen. Eventually we got the message that they were going to use the fishing rod to cast a lead weight over the water and use the fishing line to pull a rope across the river. Once the rope was secured, they would tow the little raft back and forth to ferry us back on their side, and safety.

The lead weight made it across with the line and the rope was attached as planned. Unfortunately, as soon as that rope hit the current, it snapped the fishing line. They made three attempts, but it broke every time. Plan "A" wasn't working. So they left.

We honestly didn't know what was going to happen to us at that point. We did have a lighter, and after taking it apart and drying it in the sun, we were able to get a fire going. Hours had now passed by since we got out of the water, but we were warm and on dry land. So as far as we were concerned, we were fine for the time being. We just thought that eventually something would happen.

And something did happen. At about two o'clock in the morning. This was in the middle of summer, and we were so far north, it was still light out. Suddenly we heard a helicopter. We turn to look and see it's the Alaska State Troopers! This is a big aircraft, and it came forward and landed right next to us! I don't know much about helicopters, but I'm guessing it has an eight-person capacity. After it landed, the copilot jumped out and ushered us inside without saying anything. We grabbed what was left of our raft, tossed it in, climbed aboard, and just like that we lift off! And start to head north. The three of us are kind of looking at each other, reading each other's mind, thinking that: "The truck is back to the south . . ." But nobody is saying anything. So I leaned up to the copilot. It was hard to hear anything over the noise of the engine and because we don't have headsets as the pilots do. So I just yell into the copilot: "You know, we've got a truck back there!" while I'm pointing south.

I didn't see it, but I'm sure he rolled his eyes. I could see him talking to the pilot in the left seat and the next thing we knew, this huge machine just kind of arched around and swung toward the south. They actually flew us up the river and right back to our truck, landing right beside it! It was like valet service!

We all jumped out of the helicopter, and that's when the trooper took some of our information. As a result, we ended up getting our names in the newspaper. I didn't even like getting my name in the paper if I scored a goal in B league hockey, but now I've got my name in it for this.

It was a pretty quiet drive back to Fairbanks. We weren't saying a whole lot. All of us were pretty dog faced. But I do remember thinking as we were driving along, "I'm alive! I'm an idiot, but I'm alive!"

We got back home to Fairbanks at around 7 o'clock in the morning. I called my parents to tell them I loved them.

Three days later, I'm still feeling bad about the whole thing. We all were. We were actually feeling bad about how stupid we are.

So I went out and bought three brand new life jackets—one for each of us. I went over to the house and gave Mark his, and he said, "Aw, thanks Chris. That was really nice. Thank you." Then I gave Eldon his. He took it and immediately he tossed it on the floor and dropped to his knees on top of it, bouncing up and down, saying: "It fits! The perfect size! This is great! Thanks Chris! This is awesome!"

Now, I'm sure you are thinking that the raft never saw water again. But actually, it did.

The very next summer, I patched the hole in it and pumped it up full of air. My parents had given me some baby ducks to raise, so I filled the raft up full of water and used it as a duck pond.

The Flaming,
Floating Ball of Death

KEN MOORE

Ken Moore is a good friend who I recruited for Dark Winter Nights, *and his story is a great example of how trouble can find you in Alaska—even in your own backyard. He told this story at a small live event we did in January 2015.—Rob Prince*

On the first warm day of spring 2011, I decided it was a great day to mow my lawn for the first time that season. I've learned over the years that the best way to get a beautiful, lush spring lawn is to cut it very short in the spring so water and nutrients can get down into the roots. So with my mower set at the lowest level, I began mowing in the front lawn. Every two or three swaths across the lawn I had to empty the bag of thatch, so I decided to empty it in a pile in my backyard.

I live in the Riverview neighborhood on the Chena River in Fairbanks. The river is about 75 feet wide by my house and we have about 150 feet of riverfront. Along the bank of the river is a few feet of natural growth of native grasses and shrubs that's meant to prevent erosion. And then we have about 30 feet of lawn between the river and house; it was a very dry lawn on that day. The lawn leads up to our large wooden deck, which is about a foot off the ground.

To say that our house was attached to a nice dry large slab of kindling disguised as a deck would not have been an exaggeration on that particular day.

I decided to stack the dry brown thatch from my mowing down by the river. At the edge of my lawn where I was stacking the clippings is a very large trophy spruce tree. It's gorgeously shaped, having grown beautifully for decades. It's just across the line into my neighbor's lawn. It's the focal point of his landscaping and is one of the centerpieces of our view of the river. So I stacked the mulch out of the way under my neighbor's tree as I finished mowing the front yard. After then mowing the side yard, I began mowing the dry brown grass in the backyard, going back and forth between the river and the house, stopping very frequently to empty the mower bag on the thatch pile under my neighbor's spruce tree. The pile of dry grass was growing so large it was quaking in the increasing steady winds. It was at least six feet tall, growing larger with each bag of dry grass added to it. And of course it was strategically close to that spruce tree to keep it off the section of lawn that still needed to be mowed.

When I was about halfway through manicuring the back lawn, the mower ran out of gas. So I opened the rear overhead garage door facing my back lawn and the river, grabbed the gas can, filled the mower with gas, and set the can on the lawn right in front of the door to my garage, which I left open. I started up the mower and mowed two or three more swaths back and forth to the river. On one of those revolutions, as I turned the mower around at the house and started back down toward the river, I was suddenly startled and stopped in my tracks. Right in front of me, ten feet from where I had just mowed, were some small flames of fire. They were little flames, but in the first several seconds of my immediate panic, I observed the flames growing into exponentially larger flames. The flames, however, encompassed only a small black circle of fire about a foot in diameter. So I thought, "No big deal." I released my grip on the lawnmower handle and the machine immediately shut off. Stepping quickly over to the ring of flames, I began stomping the fire with my boots to extinguish it. After my first couple stomps, I realized this was totally the wrong thing to do. Every time I stomped the fire in the dry dusty grass and thatch, each flame under my foot turned into several small torpedoes of flying burning thatch that immediately ignited several more fires, spreading into a suddenly much larger fire. And believe it or not, something told me this procedure did not seem to be working out real well.

I screamed to my wife, who was in the house, "Come! Grab some buckets!" After one look, now in a rush of panic matching mine, she ran through the open garage and grabbed some buckets. Somehow she had the presence of mind to see someone walking by the front of our house on Riverview Drive—a young gentleman. She yelled for him to come help us. On a full-out adrenaline rush, the three of us began to run back and forth from the river to the lawn, scooping and dumping the water on the small fires, which had now become a massive lawn fire pushed by stiff winds. The little voice of reason in my head shouted that we were losing this battle at a much faster pace than our legs were moving to address it.

Now, just to make things all the more interesting, the winds were not blowing briskly just in one direction. The river acts as a wind tunnel; when the wind blows down the curves of the river, it creates a swirling whirlwind effect. You got it—our once small fire was now dozens of converging fires simultaneously going all directions more quickly than we could blink an eye in the heavy smoke. Do you wonder how can a lawn burn so prolifically? Let me tell you. It's the same concept as a forest fire when the wind is blowing and the fire gets extremely hot. The flames spread at lightning speed along the tops of the trees. Well, I'll tell you something I quickly found out that spring day: dry lawn grass does exactly the same thing. So now we had ourselves a doozy of a lawn grass forest fire, out of control with no hope of containment in sight. As we continued to dip water and throw water, it was more than obvious through the flying sparks that we had lost this game. The fire was spreading in all directions simultaneously. Toward the river, toward the six-foot-tall thatch pile underneath my neighbor's pristine centerpiece spruce tree, and toward the neatly aligned kindling we called a deck . . . attached to our house, of course. In just moments the fire had completely escaped our grasp.

Without thinking another thought, I grabbed my cell phone from my pocket and dialed 911. Excruciatingly long moments after I hung up, I heard the sirens. By this time the fire had spread into the wild area of long dry prairie grass and tall brush along the river. Thus the flames were no longer only those of a lawn grass fire. They were flames shooting eight to ten feet high—crackling and blowing in the wind as they consumed everything within their greedy reach.

Though time seemed to stand still, the flames did not. Within minutes, the first fire truck came screaming down Riverview, lurching to a halt in front of the house. In a snap or two, the firefighters began hosing the fire. Oh, did I mention that by this time, the fire had reached my thatch pile under the tree and monster flames were beginning to hungrily lap up the thatch?

The firefighters were up to the task and quickly brought the situation under control, putting out the fire. By some not so small miracle, the tree was salvaged from the inferno under its branches. Kudos to Fairbanks Fire Department for their courtesy and efficiency. After they rolled their hoses we stood together catching our breath. The captain exclaimed, "Wow! That was really, really close to turning into a major disaster." The fire had literally spread to within a couple feet of the gas can waiting to explode into the open garage door. The flames had also reached the deck and were beginning to chase the long grass underneath the dry wood deck boards.

With the fire now extinguished, there was just one last thing to sort out: what to do with the massive six-foot smoldering pile of thatch? Take it apart and spread it out, risking a restart of the fire? Just leave it there to smolder? Suddenly, in a moment of a seeming genius thought, one firefighter suggested they just shove the entire smoldering pile into the river where it would, they presumed, harmlessly sink and drown itself out. Problem solved.

So, using my rakes, they pushed the entire large thatch pile into the Chena River, intentionally breaking it into smaller chunks of smoldering grass as they did so. You will recall that the Chena meanders its way through the city of Fairbanks. Mission accomplished, the firefighters boarded their trucks and drove away as smoldering piles of thatch bobbed their way down the river. As their red trucks disappeared down Riverview Drive to the south, there raced into view a yellow state forestry department truck from the north—the kind fully decked out with firefighting equipment. The truck abruptly stopped in front of our house and an officer got out quickly with a determined look and posture that screamed without words, "Someone's in deep trouble for this one." I later learned the forestry department had been sitting up on a hill on the north side of town where they could overlook the entire Fairbanks valley. Watching for smoke or fire anywhere in the dangerously dry valley was their mission on this day, when a total burning ban had been issued.

Upon seeing my plume of smoke and then spotting my Riverview fire, they followed the smoke signal, arriving just after the Fairbanks Fire Department had turned the corner out of sight.

Upon jumping purposefully out of his official yellow vehicle, the state officer stomped around my house with his citation book in hand. He was ready to write a ticket to fine this law-breaking home-owner who was burning illegally . . . so he thought. Pen in hand, he walked across my back lawn and firmly stated, "Sir! Did you not know that there is a burning ban today?"

"Yes, sir," I replied, "I know there's a burning ban."

"Then what in the hell are you doing burning your grass?"

Without hesitation, I said, "Sir, wait, wait, you don't understand. I can tell you how this happened." His look of skepticism was unmistakable as he glared holes through me. "Sir, I was mowing my lawn and the lawnmower started the fire."

Upon hearing my explanation, his look was one of total disbelief as he readjusted the pen in hand, now ready for sure to write a ticket. Sensing his utter disgust at my explanation, I went on quickly, "Sir, no, come look!" I urged the reluctant officer over to the lawnmower that was still sitting where I had suddenly abandoned it upon discovering the fire. The flames, however, had since burned all around the mower, leaving it in the middle of black charred lawn. Impulsively, I moved it and tipped it on its side. Under the deck of the lawnmower was a clump of still smoldering grass. As if programmed by fate to save my butt, a gust of wind caused the ball of grass to spontaneously burst into flame.

With shock and embarrassment fully encompassing his face, the officer took a step back and put his citation book back in his pocket, apparently convinced that I was not the criminal of which he had been so certain. As we then stood in awe of the entire bizarre situation, his angst suddenly turned to amusement. Now on the level of trusted friends, he and I began musing how on earth my entire place . . . and the spruce tree . . . did not go up in flames powered by an exploding gas can and kindled by the recently refinished deck. After the officer realized I wasn't intentionally starting fires on that dry day, I began to recall with him the blow-by-blow details of the inferno, including the finishing touch by the fire department, the brilliant decision to shove the smoking pile of thatch into the river.

"They did *what*?!" he asked. He immediately surveyed the floating bundles of burning thatch, still within view as they bobbed down the river. Gasping for his next breath as he mumbled and swore, he urgently radioed his team, telling them to get a boat into the water ASAP. He told them where to launch the boat downriver. He yelled into the phone for them to get on the river as soon as you blankety-blank can, come up the river, and look for smoldering, flaming bogs of grass before they floated to the river's edge, igniting other tinder dry shorelines, causing other infernos. They heeded the officer's request and were on the water promptly. The captain anxiously waited until the boat pulled up on our riverbank a few minutes later. The officers in the boat assured their partner that they had in fact broken up and extinguished all the smoldering bogs.

Well, dear reader, I gained new friends that day and realized anew how well the folks in our community serve their citizens to keep us from danger . . . or should I say rescue us once danger's fangs have enveloped us in their vicious grip.

There's been a lot of news in the last few months about the legalization of marijuana. Now we, the upstanding citizens of Alaska, have voted for the legalization of such. But at the end of the day on May 14, 2011, I decided that smoking weed and grass is not such a great idea after all.

It's Not a Coffin

ERIC STEVENS

I feel like if I had 100 Erics I could take over the world of storytelling. He is a wonderfully natural storyteller whose story still makes me smile to this day. It certainly makes me think twice about eating A-1 steak sauce. He shared this delightful story about marital relations in times of trouble at our April 2016 live event in Fairbanks.—Rob Prince

It's 2003 and my wife and I have decided to celebrate our second anniversary by taking an eleven-mile ski trip into Tolovana Hot Springs to stay in a rustic cabin. So me, my wife, and our dog make our way to Tolovana in our trusty old blue Subaru.

Along the dirt road to Tolovana, there's a wide spot on the left where you can pull in—that's the trailhead. It is always windy at that trailhead. I've only been there three times, but trust me, it's always windy; a sample size of three shows 100 percent accuracy. We park the car and get all of our gear out, including our skis. We put our gear into a little toboggan to pull behind us. If you pay over $100 for one of these things at a fancy ski shop, it's called a "pulk." If you go to a grocery store, it's called a sled and you get it for $10.

As we leave that parking lot, the trail goes straight downhill. I'm thinking, "This is so much fun! Get away, dog! You're getting in our way!" We crash once in a while, but that's okay. Then there's this flat, cold part of the trail, and then we go back uphill and there is this knob of terrain where it's too brutal for trees to grow. It's like a windy moonscape. There's nothing living here and you just try to get through that part as quick as you can because of the harsh wind. Then you come back down and there you are at the hot springs eleven miles later.

We have rented this little cabin. It's rustic. Rustic means no water, no electricity, no heat other than what you create yourself by firing up the wood stove. There's a Coleman stove, so if you bring some of your own fuel you can cook things by going out and getting water out of a little hole. We get things squared away. I'm unpacking the sleeping bags to put on the little bunks. Then Deanne says, "We're going to have dinner." This is an anniversary dinner she pulls out. It was in my pulk and I didn't even know it. She's clever in that way. And there's steak! We're going to have steak! And a bottle of champagne! This is gonna be so much fun! So she whips it together while I'm unpacking. Then I don't do much but sit there and wait for food. Then, okay, here's steak!—by candlelight even! Our anniversary dinner!

Then Deanne says, "Oh, Eric, would you like anything with your steak?" and I answer hopefully, "Is there asparagus?" "No," she says. "I mean, salt and pepper." I'm from North Dakota, so that's where it stops when it comes to condiments. You've got to draw the line because there could be moral corruption if you go beyond the salt and pepper stage. But then Deanne sees on the windowsill in this little cabin a half-empty little bottle of A-1 steak sauce with the nice little bit of crust around the cap. Deanne says, "Well, how about some steak sauce?" and I say, "Well . . . no. I'm good," remembering the North Dakota thing. "No, I better not. I don't want to get too crazy." She says, "Alright, suit yourself," and puts it on her own steak. "This is pretty good steak sauce!" So we have dinner. That's great. The dog gets dinner. Then we go out and soak in the hot tubs for a little bit. That's fun. We go back to the cabin. We're going to finish the champagne. This has been the greatest little anniversary trip ever.

A lot of my life is about being oblivious. I don't notice things until afterwards when they're explained to me and then I go, "Ooohh, yeah!" Well, it turns out the next morning that Deanne doesn't feel so good when she wakes up. So what do you have to have when you're out camping? You've got to have instant oatmeal! That's what makes the world go round. I love oatmeal! Bring it on! Deanne eats her oatmeal. There's some leftovers, so I eat those all up. I've got to wax up the skis and get ready to go. Meanwhile, Deanne discreetly, subtly, and without my knowledge goes to the outhouse and . . . *blaaaaaah*! Return to sender.

Breakfast is all gone. She's got rid of that oatmeal and she's sick! She is in a bad way, but she comes out of the outhouse acting like everything is fine, so I don't have any clue what's going on . . . Okay, got our skis waxed up; the pulks look good. We're ready to go. It's eleven miles back to the car. It's just starting to get light outside. Perfect timing.

We hit the trail, head uphill. When we get to that knobby moonscape on the top, I'm thinking, "Okay, what I've learned about being outside for a whole, long day of activity like this is you've got to drink water before you're thirsty. You've got to eat food before you're hungry. You do not want to crash aerobically. You do not want to fall behind on this stuff." So I say when we get the top, "How about a snack? You want some M&Ms or something?" Deanne goes, "Uh, uh, no, I don't really like M&Ms." So I go, "Okay" and munch, munch, munch them all down. "Want some water?" I ask. "We got some water. You should drink water." And she says, "No, I'm not thirsty." I say, "What? You've got to drink . . . here, drink some water. Come on!" And she goes, "Okay . . ." and she takes a couple sips of water and hands me back the water bottle. I'm putting it away when I hear this sound. I look up and Deanne goes, "*Ummm-bllll-aaaaahhhh*" and it's all gone! I say, "What's going on?" and she says, "I don't feel good . . . Earlier this morning I couldn't keep my breakfast down. I'm nauseous and I'm tired and I just want to take a rest." We're up at the part of the trail where there is no resting. This is the moonscape part and the northeast wind is fifteen to twenty-five miles per hour. We have got to keep moving! You've got to keep going! And the car . . . We're not going to wait for tectonic drift to take us to the car! We've got to go! I'm starting to get a little worried about this.

"Okay, let's go, let's go," I say. I'm going to ski behind Deanne in case she wants to stop. She keeps slowing down, so I give her this friendly little encouragement called a nudge. "Okay, let's go! Gotta keep going!" She goes, "*Ah-wah-we-wah*, whatever." I nudge her again, but she keeps slowing down. I go, "Come on!" and I'm watching the time. I'm German anyway, so it's all about time! Come on! At one point I say, "Come on, Deanne, we have *got to go!*" And she turns around and yells, "*Quit pushing me!*" And that's when I think, "We *are* going to die out here . . . It's not working out."

We get down to the bottom part of the trail and I come up with this bright idea. "Tell you what, Deanne, just unbuckle your pulk and we'll leave it here. We'll go these last few miles back to the car." And I don't tell her this next part but I tell myself, "And the car *will* start." Then I tell her, "And then you can sit in the car with the dog, get all warmed up, and I'll go back and be a superhero and grab your pulk and ski back with that and then we'll load up and go back to town." "Okay, great plan," she says.

So we get up to the top—up, up, up, up—and we come around to the right and there's the parking lot and, sure enough, there's the car with snow drifted all over on one side because of the wind. We find the keys and get into the car and I pray to Japanese-American collaboration . . . and it starts! Yes! There you go! There are no plug-ins up there to plug in the engine block heater, so we had to just hope the engine wouldn't freeze and seize up. I say, in my superhero voice, "Deanne, everything is working out wonderfully. You stay here. I will retrieve your gear!" I'm feeling about twelve feet tall.

I ski down, grab the pulk, turn around, and come back. It's slower going back with the weight, but I get up there. I come around to the right, arrive at the parking lot, and . . . there's no car! There is just a bare piece of snow-covered gravel. If there was a car there, you would see it! Nevertheless, I turn around to look for it. "Where's the Subaru?! It's gone!" And then I think, "You know what, maybe I've really pushed her one too many times! She might be in the car right now thinking, 'You know what, we've been married for a couple of years. You know, we gave it the good try.'"

I know that after two years we have gone from the "I love you" phase of our relationship to the "I love you *anyway*" phase. Maybe I've just gone over the edge of that cliff and she's thinking to herself, "You know what? Screw him! This way it will look like an accident. I'll let Mother Nature do the dirty work out there. Besides, he deserves to suffer just a little as he goes. I'll tell the police that I was so delusional in my flu and food poisoning that I thought he was in the car with me and I just drove away! He's not very talkative. He's from North Dakota. I thought he was with me!"

Well . . . I know you've got to drink before you're thirsty, you've got to eat before you're hungry, so now I'm thinking, "I've got to find shelter before I die of frostbite!" So there are these two pulks. There's the one I brought up earlier and Deanne's pulk I just brought up. There are sleeping bags in the pulks, so I empty all the stuff out of them. The vision I have in mind is that I'm going to make a clamshell out of these two pulks and I'm going to climb in there. To be clear, the image at work here is *clamshell*. It is not *coffin*, although there could be some overlap . . .

I'm getting ready and I'm positioning this clamshell so I can open it up and peek through the crack for cars as they—maybe, hopefully—go by. Then I can close them and go shields down. I'm getting ready to get into the clamshell when, sure enough, from the east in the darkness are these distant headlights blazing through the wisps of snow. I think, "There is something coming! Okay, I'm going to jump out and flag this guy down and I want to flag him down *urgently* but not *crazy* urgent, like 'Blaaaa-haaaah!' because then he would get freaked out and either keep going or run me over. I'm going to be *appropriately assertive*."

The car is coming and it starts to slow down. Good news, good news. And . . . it's a blue Subaru wagon! It's Deanne! In my coolest tone I say, "Hey, Deanne! What's going on?" She says, "Oh, you know what, it was so cold and windy up here and the car was so cold from sitting there so long that it wasn't generating any heat. It was an endothermic combustion and I was just shivering in there. The dog was shivering in there. So I wanted to get the car under power, so I drove down the road for about twenty minutes and came back." And I lie, "Yeah, that's what I thought you probably did." So we get everything loaded up and head home. The dog's wagging his tail.

And so I've learned that there are times when you can nudge a loved one, but maybe it's good to know also when not to push too hard. We're still alive! We're still married!

Starving off the Land

PHILLIP CHARETTE

Phillip's story is a wonderful window into the thinking of a twenty-something in Alaska who is full of a drive for adventure but very short on experience. That's typically an extremely dangerous combination up here, but thankfully in his case it's merely a recipe for a hilarious backwoods skiing debacle. I interviewed him back in 2016 about his experience for our radio show and podcast.—Rob Prince

Back in the 1980s, Phillip Charette and two of his college friends were feeling a little envious of students who are going to nice, warm places for spring break. So they decided to have their own adventure. Their plan was to spend the weekend in the White Mountains here in Alaska. They'd ski in twenty miles to a secluded state-maintained cabin and hunt grouse, ptarmigan, and rabbits to supplement the food they carried in. Rob Prince interviewed Phillip for this story.

PHIL: My roommate had spent time in the wilderness so I assumed that he knew we were skiing about twenty miles and that he knew what he was doing. He was in charge of all the food and water. It wasn't until the night before we left that I realized all the food he had purchased was canned, so our packs each weighed about seventy pounds. That's without the water! So he decided to take some weight out. He took the water out, thinking we would just fill it up when we got there—but then he forgot all about it.

The first part of the trip, leaving off the Elliott Highway, is an uphill ski to the top of a ridge. He had the gorp ready.

ROB: Good old raisins and peanuts.

PHIL: Exactly. So we had what we needed. We packed ourselves up, we got all the gear, and I said, "Do you have the water?" And he said, "Yeah, don't worry about it. It's all taken care of." However, in the confusion of getting everything together, he forgot the water. So we started going up the hill, up the hill. The temperature was roughly twenty above in the heat of the day and twenty below at night—a huge temperature range.

When we started skiing up there, we were really chilled and we just focused on warming up. We skied uphill to get to the summit. Once we're at the summit we were eating more of the gorp and, with the saltiness of it and everything, we were getting really thirsty. I asked my roommate, "Where is the water?" . . . and there was no water. My roommate said, "Well, I thought you had it." I said, "No, you said you put it in our packs and you forgot."

One of the guys who was with us was an unseasoned skier and he was having a really difficult time. After you get to the summit, there's a long downhill run into the valley. We decided the people with the least experience should go first, so we let the inexperienced guy go. We watched him head down the hill. About 100 yards in front of us, he lost his balance and went face-first into a snowbank. We saw his feet swinging back and forth in the air; he looked like a beetle stuck on its back. The weight of his backpack shoved him headfirst way into a snowbank—he was stuck and totally couldn't breathe.

We said, "Oh, my God, oh, my God!" dropped our packs, and rushed as fast as we could to him. He was buried in about six feet of snow and by the time we skied up to him, his feet were just . . . jerking, like he was running out of air. Then his legs stopped jerking, and we said, "Uh-oh . . ." There was no time to dig, so we just grabbed him by his pack and pulled him out. He gasped for air. His face was blue. We were really worried, but he got his breath back. All of that was about a half-hour ordeal.

We managed to get down the rest of the hill with no further drama. At the bottom of the hill, we took a break. The guy who went headfirst into the snow was getting super dehydrated. All of a sudden his eyes rolled toward the back of his head and he fell backwards. We said, "Oh, crap!" We got his skis off and all of his gear off. He's lying there on the ground mumbling but all we could make out was "Mama." We said, "Oh, no. This is not good." He opened his eyes, and they were cross-eyed. He was seriously dehydrated.

Finally he said, "Go on, guys! You can make it! You know it's not that far. Go on without me! You guys are great friends and I'm going to miss you!" We were thinking, "Oh, my God." He was serious. He thought he was going to die. We were panicking now. We had to do something.

My roommate had the great idea of making a fire to melt some snow. This meant that the water had ash and charcoal and all kinds of bits of junk in it, but finally we were able to get this guy some water. He drank it and when he looked at us and smiled we could see big chunks of ash and stuff in his teeth. He said, "Man, you guys go ahead. You can still make it." I answered, "No, we are not going on without you. I know there is water up ahead. There has got to be water."

Sure enough, 100 yards from where I said there had to be water, there was water. We filled up all of our containers and continued on our journey, because we had another fifteen-plus miles to go.

ROB: So you *continued* going toward the cabin? Why didn't you go home?

PHIL: We were out for an adventure and dammit, we were going to have one! There were some closer cabins on the map, so we figured we could at least make it to them. We could decide at that point what we were going to do.

ROB: So, in the first five miles of your trip, one man has almost died twice.

PHIL: Yes.

ROB: And that's not enough for you to decide to call it quits?

PHIL: He did not want to call it quits! He's not from Alaska. He said, "Come on, this is a once-in-a-lifetime journey, I'll never get to do this again!"

ROB: Yeah, because your life's about to end!

PHIL: By the time it started getting dark, we realized that we weren't going to make it to the LeFevre cabin. We knew there was an emergency shelter close by, but we were told there were Boy Scouts staying there that night.

ROB: At least you know they would be prepared!

PHIL: Yeah! We figured maybe they wouldn't show up and we could stay at that cabin. By then, the temperature had dropped drastically, and we were all sopping wet from sweating—even my experienced roommate started to get cold. So we went into the emergency cabin. It was really small, only about four by four feet wide! Absolutely tiny. When we lay down in it, we had to have our knees bent because it was too small to stretch out in.

ROB: I don't know if *cabin* is the right word for this. Maybe *shed*?

PHIL: It's a shelter. It's like a shed.

ROB: What temperature would you guess it was?

PHIL: At that point the temperature dropped down to around twenty below.

ROB: Okay.

PHIL: We knew that we couldn't travel in those temperatures. We figured if the Boy Scouts showed up, it was going to be tight because we are not leaving!

ROB: [*Laughs*] Three college students and eleven Boy Scouts, in a sixteen-square-foot shed! Sounds like a bar joke to me.

The Boy Scouts never showed up. So after a night in their luxurious accommodation, the three guys felt much better and decided to continue on their trek to their ultimate destination, the LeFevre cabin.

PHIL: The unseasoned skier fell again a number of times. Once he lost control and ran into a tree, so we had to doctor him up again.

ROB: I feel so bad for this guy!

PHIL: We were really close to the LeFevre cabin. When we got within sight of it, I skied forward and dropped off my pack, then skied back to him and picked up his so he didn't have to carry it, because he was done. He had nothing left to give.

The three friends spent the first night in the cabin battling with a broken woodstove and a mice infestation, conditions that continued to test the mettle of their greenhorn companion.

PHIL: The first night my inexperienced friend had a hard time because he didn't like mice. I think he ended up sleeping on the countertop. Then we started running out of food. We had the dishes my roommate had hauled in. The main one was called "Chicken in a Can." It was a whole chicken in a can! Just stuffed in there, bones and all.

After we finished off two chickens in a can, we needed to go out hunting. We were told there were ptarmigan, grouse, rabbits . . . you know, something out there, so my roommate and I went hunting. Our inexperienced friend stayed in the cabin. He was not interested in coming out. He said, "No, go ahead, you guys. I'm okay. I'll be fine here." He sequestered himself in the cabin and said, "I'll take care of the fire."

So he kept the fire going and the cabin warmed. We took our shotguns to go look for birds, rabbits, and whatever, but we found nothing. So we had no food. We ate the last of our crackers, the last of our sardines, the last of everything we had. That night we had to decide whether to go or stay. We had planned on another few days in the cabin, but now we had no food, and we knew it would take a lot of energy to ski the twenty miles back out of the place because we had that huge summit to get over to get out to the Elliott Highway.

ROB: It's a lot of work to nearly kill yourself.

PHIL: It is!

It became apparent that the inexperienced skier was not going to make it all the way back to the car on his own, so they all skied to the base of the summit and Phil and his roommate skied on to their beater car without him. They planned to drop their gear and then return to help their friend make it back.

PHIL: We didn't have the car engine block heater plugged in because there was no place to plug it in out there in the middle of nowhere. When we tried to start the frozen engine, it was like, "*Dddd-rrrr*, click, click, click, *drrr*." We had no heat, no food, but we did have the water my roommate had forgotten! But it was frozen . . . My roommate and I figured we needed energy, so we started scrounging around in the car. We dug into the glove compartment and found this very old bottle of blackberry brandy that wasn't frozen. My roommate found a stick of gum. Then he went into his toolbox and at the very bottom of it, under all the tools, was a pack of ramen noodles. So all we had to give us the energy we needed to ski up the hill, grab our friend, and come back was this blackberry brandy and a super old pack of ramen.

ROB: Don't forget the stick of gum.

PHIL: Yeah, the stick of gum. I just wasn't into that! As for this package of ramen—I couldn't even tell if it was Top Ramen because the tools had rusted over the top of the package. You could not even read the word *ramen* on the package. It had been in his toolbox for who knows how long. My roommate handed me half of the dried cake of ramen. We both chewed on the dried noodles, sprinkling the contents of the seasoning packet into our mouths, and chased this delicacy with the blackberry brandy.

We were both shaky and tired, and we still had not gotten the car to start. We did have the camping stove in the car. We lit that up and put it under the car, hoping we wouldn't set it on fire. We waited a few minutes and monitored it. We had a fire extinguisher ready just in case. We put a sleeping bag over the hood of the car to try to warm it up. Eventually we managed to get the car to go, "*Rrr-rrr*" and we were getting hopeful. After about twenty minutes, we finally got the car fired up. We let the motor run to let the car warm up.

Then we thought, "Oh, gosh, we have to go back and get Jim!" The temperature was dropping, so we knew we had to keep the car running while we were gone. It would be nice and warm by the time we get back. So we started gearing up. My roommate took another shot of brandy. I took another shot of brandy. Then we looked up the mountain. On the ridge, way up top, we saw one of those long-track snow machines. On the back of it there was this figure, bouncing like a ragdoll, not holding on, but just lying there. We couldn't figure out what we were seeing at first. Turned out a Park Service guy had rescued our friend, who was at this point pretty delirious. The ranger had given him some water, but he was still out of it. That park ranger was not very happy with us! He let us know how dangerous it was to do what we had done and that we had better not let this happen ever again!

We got our companion back into the vehicle, got him warmed up, and that was the end of that part of the trip.

The Epic Trade

STEVE NEUMETH

Steve has a million amazing stories from Alaska. The problem is finding the ones he'll agree to tell. Fortunately, I was able to get him on stage to tell this story about a man's love for his wife, his wife's love for her goose, and the goose's disdain for the man. He told this story at our April 2015 live event in Fairbanks.—Rob Prince

I've got a great wife and I love her. And if you really love your wife, you'll do just about anything for her—as this story proves.

We raised animals: ducks, chickens, pigs, sheep, goats . . . and then I made the error of buying my wife two Toulouse geese, a male and a female. We named the male Cinder and the female Ella. They were very cute geese and they grew bigger and bigger . . . and then they grew *big*. Big geese are like dogs when they do "their thing" in the morning. They make big piles . . . These geese loved my wife so much. They were not just farm animals, they were pets. They always wanted to meet her at the door, so they would waddle up the three steps to my deck and wait at the door for her to come out. In the process they would leave me things to clean up. I love my wife and she never really wanted to clean up after the animals, so I did it. They would leave piles all around the deck and I would come out with a putty knife and scrape them off. In the winter they would freeze solid and I would have to chisel them off. And if you've ever had Vibram soles and stepped in goose poop, you will know it's quite an experience trying to get them clean.

Unfortunately one day a stray dog came into the yard and killed Cinder. We were all in mourning, wearing black for a while. But you know, life went on, except that Ella was really lonely. She didn't have her guy. So she hung out on the deck all the time. It was really a mess. I built her a big house. I put a heater in it. I put hay in it. She would have nothing to do with it. I put a battery pad heater in it. No use. She still hung out on the deck all the time.

One Wednesday in the winter my wife was getting ready to go on a big trip to California to visit her mom. She was very excited. When I dropped her off at the airport she said, "Now you make sure you take care of my last goose. I need to be certain that I can trust you . . ." I interrupted, "I got this goose *covered*. No problem! Food, water, everything." So I said good-bye to my wife, came home, and checked on Ella that night. Everything was good. Thursday morning when I left for work the goose was fine. I came home that evening and went out on the deck to check. Her food was fine. Her water was fine. I had a pad under the water to make sure it stayed thawed so the goose could drink.

Of course the goose was on the deck, but I was so tired of kicking her off the deck that I just said, "Forget it. Stay there if you want." I figured live and let live. It was thirty below zero at the time. It was *cold*. I went inside and cooked dinner.

Friday night I came home from work and walked out on the deck. The goose was on the deck as usual. What was funny was that she was in the same place I'd seen her the day before . . . I thought that was odd. She would always move a little bit when I came over. So I walked over to the goose and she was like a statue. There was a ring of solid poop around her. She was frozen solid to the deck! I mean *solid*. I thought, "Oh, God, this is my chance to be done with this goose! It's thirty below zero, I'm not going to get this goose off the deck. There's only one way to resolve this—I've got to do the goose in. This is my golden opportunity to finally be done cleaning poop off my deck."

I called my wife and said, "Sweetheart, I am so sorry to tell you this, but the goose is frozen to the deck in its own poop and there's no way I'm going to get this goose out. Listen, I just can't get this thing off." She said, "Oh, God! I understand. And she's lived a long life. She's probably sad and lonely because she doesn't have her mate anymore. Go ahead."

So I whipped out my .22 pistol and went out there . . . and that goose turned and looked at me as only a female goose can do. If this had been a male goose, I would have just shot him. But she looked at me with the softest eyes and pleaded with me, and I thought, "Oh, man, I can't do this . . ." So I went into the garage, got a short-handled sledgehammer and a spade chisel, and started to beat at the frozen poop ring around this goose. I pounded. All of a sudden the goose gave way and flipped over. I grabbed hold of her, kicked the garage door handle, and steered her into the heated garage. I set her on my knee, put a plug in the slop sink, and filled it up with warm water.

Neither one of us knew what was going to happen. As I set that goose down in the warm water, the stench of heated goose poop was beyond anything either one of us could handle. She had her head as far out of the sink as she could get it and was gasping for air. It was just a mess and I had to put my hand in that poop soup and pull the plug. I repeated this process three times until finally one of her feet came free and she started paddling in a circle. It was just . . . it was just . . . filthy! But my mission was not yet complete. I filled the sink up with warm water again, and finally the second leg came out. I could tell she was thinking, "Oh . . . man! This is great!" She was doing circles and then she started diving to wash herself off! This goose has a six-foot wingspan! So we are both wearing the contents of that slop sink. I cleaned it out again, filled it up one last time with warm water, and she dove underneath there and she just . . . Aww . . . she was *ecstatic*. I just let her take a bath at that point. I had already taken a kind of bath—I was covered in green poop.

Then I thought, "Okay, wait a minute . . . Now what do I do? I've got a soaking wet goose, it's thirty below zero, she's in my garage . . ." So I got a great idea: hay! I got some hay and put it in the back of my truck, then fetched the goose from the sink. By the way, she was an angel to me throughout this nightmare. She didn't like me very much because she was kind of hip to the fact that I was the bad guy—she knew I had killed her babies a few times. But at this moment she didn't make a move. I scooped up this wet thing, carried her to the back of the truck, and plopped her in the hay. I got her a big bowl of food and water. She hadn't eaten in three days because she'd just been sitting there pooping in her pile, so she just *consumed* that food. I said, "Okay, you're in. Go to sleep. In the morning I'll let you out."

The next morning I opened the garage door. She had already exited the truck and, after having eaten that whole bowl of food, she'd produced what made it look like I'd had a sled dog team parked in my garage. Poop was everywhere. So I opened up the door and I said, "Out." She looked at me and, I swear, we had a moment. Goose and man had a connection. She looked at me and just . . . I don't know . . . there was something there between us. But that was all. It stopped right there. She waddled out the door, made a right turn, went up three steps to the deck, and parked her butt right by the door. So I thought, "You know, live and let live."

My wife didn't know that I had saved the goose. She thought the goose was dead. So when she got home and Ella waddled over to her, the two of them were overjoyed. This goose loved my wife. And so did I.

Incidentally, as a husband, you can use an event like this for great, great, great, great things down the road. We need collateral to trade what we can, and a major, epic service such as I provided is worth a lot.

That's a Big Bear!

JAN HANSCOM

Jan's story is a great example of how trouble can not only find you when you venture outside in Alaska–it will deliver trouble right into your house like some kind of life-threatening DoorDash doppelganger. She shared her story with me during an interview for our radio show in 2016.–Rob Prince

It was July 27–my wedding anniversary. I wanted to make a special dinner for my husband, so I started some ribs cooking in a pot while I cleaned up the kitchen. I ended up with a bag of trash, so I put it out in the entryway. In Alaska, we have "arctic entries," which are not unique to Alaska and are generally small rooms that people use to take off their coats and boots so that they do not trek snow into the house. And these rooms also keep cold air from rushing into the house.

Our cat went outside when I put the trash out, and I thought I'd leave the door open because the cat was bound to want to come back in pretty soon. So to kill a few minutes I went up our spiral staircase to the loft to check my email. Well, you know how it is when you get on the computer–you kind of lose track of time. Gradually I became aware there was a noise coming from the entryway. I thought, "Oh, there's a neighbor's dog getting in my trash!" So I ran down the spiral stairs and banged on the door–it's a steel door with no windows– yelling, "*Go home! Go home!*"

Then I opened the door to see if the dog was gone. I looked up . . . and up . . . and slammed the door. That was *not* a dog. That was a *bear*. Then I thought, "Maybe I didn't see that right. It was dark out there." I reached for the light switch. And then I froze. Wait . . . why was it dark out there in the middle of summer? As I was holding the door closed with both hands—a door that has no lock on it whatsoever—I realized that the only way *out* of the entryway was through this door and into my house. The bear must have accidentally pushed closed the other door to the outside and now it was stuck in my entryway. I spun around, grabbed my cell phone off the table, and ran back up the stairs. I figured I had just shown this bear the only way out of his little prison, and that was *into my house*. I called 911.

"Yes, ma'am. What is your emergency? Police, fire, or ambulance?"

I was confused. "I don't know! I don't know! There's a bear stuck in my entryway!"

The operator said, "Okay, I will forward you to the state troopers."

The next guy said, "Yes, ma'am, what is your emergency?"

"I don't know! There's a bear stuck in the entryway!"

"Oh, I'm sorry. All of our Fish and Wildlife officers are on a search and rescue right now."

I was beginning to panic. "So what am I supposed to do about the bear in my entryway?!"

"Umm . . . I can send the state troopers to your house."

"Yes!" I said. "That's fine. That's fine. That's good. Send the troopers!"

"Is there anyone coming to visit you this afternoon?" he asked.

"Umm, no. Not that I know of."

"Because," he went on, "we wouldn't want anyone to open the door by mistake."

I said, "Okay, from the loft, where I am, I can open the window and step onto the roof of the arctic entryway. Then if anyone were to come by, I could tell them, 'Don't open the door! There's a bear in the entryway!'" I took up my position on the roof.

"Okay ma'am, is everything alright? Are you safe right now?"

I said, "Well . . . yes . . . I suppose . . . I mean, I'm safe *right now*."

He said, "Okay, then. Call me back if anything changes," and he hung up.

"What does he mean, *if anything changes*?!" I thought. "Like if I'm being eaten by a bear?"

I've called 911 only a couple other times in my whole life and every other time they stayed on the line with me until help arrived. But this guy hung up! So I'm standing there on the roof of the entryway, holding my phone, very confused and not knowing what to do while listening to the bear down below banging and crashing into stuff.

Not sure what else to do, I called my husband. "Hey! There's a bear stuck in the entryway!"

He said, "I'll be right home!"

"Oh, no, don't worry. The police are coming. They will take care of it."

"Ahh, okay," he said, and then *he* hung up.

A total of forty-five minutes went by from the time I started this whole process of panicking about the bear in the entryway to the time the first cop car, a big SUV, came down the road. The cop got out and, just like on TV, crouched behind the car door. He looked up at me standing on the roof and called, "Ma'am, is the bear still here?"

I thought, "Why would I still be up here if it wasn't in there?" and said, "*Yes!*" pointing down at the entryway roof. "It's stuck in the entryway!"

He said, "Okay" and got out this big gun from the console of the SUV. He walked over and looked at the entryway for a moment, then he said, "So, we have to open the door . . ."

I said, "*Yes!* You have to open the door!"

At that point, another state trooper cruiser came sailing up the driveway. This guy seemed very young, perhaps just out of trooper school. He had on his little flat-brimmed trooper hat and his trousers were creased really nice. He looked sharp. He walked over to the first guy and said, "We have to open that door!" Well, at least we were all in agreement about that.

The first guy said, "We'd better be prepared. If we open the door, the bear may charge." The young guy started to get the pistol out of his holster, but the first guy scoffed, "Put that away and go get a real gun!" So the young guy went back to his car, got his big shotgun from the console, and walked back.

In the meantime two more cars came sailing up my driveway. Now I had four trooper cars in the yard, all the troopers looking at the door going, "We have to open the door!" Finally, one said, "I'll open the door!" The other three went up the steep hill and spread out—all pointing their big guns at my house.

The trooper was about to open the door when one of the others shouted, "*Wait a minute*! Shouldn't we have a plan? Which way are you going to run? We don't want to shoot you!" So they all got back together and chatted for a little bit. One of the guys looked up at me and asked, "Ma'am, are you the only person home?"

"Uh, yes. I'm the only one here."

"Oh, good! We wouldn't want to shoot anyone inside by mistake."

Now I was thinking, "Oh, no! They're going to shoot my house up like a drive-by shooting!"

They dispersed again. The guy turned the doorknob . . . and nothing happened. He called to the others, "The door won't open!"

I thought, "The door opens *in* and the bear has been there for at least forty-five minutes. All the stuff in the entryway is now all over the floor, everything from the garbage to skis and shovels, so when they try to open the door, it's running into all that stuff and it won't open. Now what do we do?"

The trooper with the hat said, "I'll get the door ram and we will bash it in!"

I said, "Wait, aren't those just meant to knock out the door latch? That won't work here."

He said, "Yeah, that probably won't work. Let's get a chainsaw."

"The chainsaws," I said, "are in the entryway."

Finally one guy found a long-handled ice chipper. It's like a straightened-out garden hoe. He started pushing the things that were blocking the door from opening further into the entryway. Then the door started to bang . . . The bear had gotten his claws around the door and was trying to pull the door open while this guy was trying to push the door in. Face-to-paws with this bear, he said, "Whoa . . . That's a big bear!" *Yes*, I thought it was a big bear too.

Then the guy who was pushing the door started running away. The bear must have pulled the door open enough that he could squeeze himself through the opening. The three guys on top of the hill were waving their arms and guns, screaming and yelling to scare the bear away. The bear turned. His eyes were so large you could see the whites of them. He was petrified. Then he went running off into the woods.

The three troopers who had arrived last just hopped into their cars and left. The first trooper said cheerily, "Okay, ma'am, that's it!" He wrote something in a little book and then off he went as well.

Still standing up there on the entryway with my heart still pounding, I said, "Bye . . . ?"

Later, the cat did come back, seemingly oblivious to what had happened in its absence.

A Bear by the Tail

RANDY BROWN

Randy's wonderful, sweet demeanor belies the fact that his left pinky toe is approximately 1,000 times more legit, OG, bush Alaskan man than I'll ever be. Frankly, I'm kind of amazed I get to live in a time when guys like Randy are still around. I think you'll feel the same way when you read his story. He shared this doozy of a story at our April 2015 live event in Fairbanks.—Rob Prince

Randy Brown is pretty much exactly what you picture when you imagine a man who could survive all on his own in the deep woods of Alaska. He grew up in New Mexico but moved to Alaska in 1975 at the age of seventeen. The following year he moved out into the deep woods and spent the next fifteen years fishing, hunting, trapping, and mushing dogs. In 1991 he moved to Fairbanks with his wife and two boys, and Fairbanks has been their home ever since.

In the mid-1970s I moved to the deep woods and spent the next fifteen years out there. I had just graduated high school in New Mexico and relocated to Alaska. Within a year I had moved out to the Upper Yukon in the stretch between Eagle and Circle. That's about a 160-mile stretch of the Yukon River. There are five tributary rivers that flow into the Yukon in that stretch, so there was a lot of country you could get to with a boat. There were about twenty different families and individuals living out in that country at the time. All of them had come from somewhere else, found some place where they were a little distant from any other neighbors, built cabins, and started living off the land. At that time there wasn't anybody to say they couldn't do that.

This was the land and the people that John McPhee wrote about in his book *Coming into the Country*. All of us living out there had some things in common: we were all living in cabins that we had fixed up or built, we all hunted and fished for our food, and we all trapped fur for our cash. We'd take our furs into Eagle in late winter, mail them down to the Seattle or Vancouver fur auctions, and sometime the next summer we'd get a check for $3,000, $5,000, $8,000, whatever, depending on how ambitious we were as trappers and what the fur prices were at the time. This would be our yearly income. We'd go to the post office, because there wasn't any bank there in Eagle, and the post office would cash the fur check and write a bunch of postal money orders. Then we'd take the money orders out to the store and buy stuff. Usually we'd spend all the fur money. Sometimes there was a little bit left over, but you didn't take it out in the woods with you because there was nothing to buy out there and nobody out in the woods had jobs. They were fully engaged in living off the land. A lot of people would only go to town once or twice a year or even just every three or four years. There were a lot of people who just stayed out in the woods.

One of the other things we all had in common was dogs. We all got around the bush with dogs. We would mush in the winter and the dogs would pack loads in the summer. These weren't the little race huskies you see around town in Fairbanks. These were monster dogs. They were 100–120 pound animals. The reason we had big dogs out there was because they had to be strong enough to break their own trails in the deep snow. Nobody was out there making trails for you. There was anywhere from fifteen to twenty miles between cabins. You didn't run across broken trails hardly ever, so if you got to mush down a broken trail, it was because you had broken it. And those big dogs were capable of moving through the deep snow, breaking trail, and working hard for us out there. They weren't very fast, but they had heavy enough fur that they could sleep without any problem at sixty below zero, which we used to have back in those days.

Because people lived a long ways from each other, there wasn't ever anybody to come and take care of your dogs when you went out to do something, right? So your dogs went with you everywhere. If you were going down to the Yukon to fish for king salmon, the dogs went with you. If you were heading up into the mountains to hunt sheep, the dogs went with you up there too, and the dogs would pack gear and stuff. If you got a sheep up in the mountains, the dogs would pack the meat out. They would have a ham of a sheep on each side and just walk away with it. It might be forty or forty-five pounds, but these big dogs could take it.

All the animals out there saw our dogs as wolves, and wolves as a pack are the most powerful predator team out there, period. Us folks with our dogs were even more powerful because we worked as a team. The dogs were really an essential part of life for us out in the woods. But as good as the dogs were, they could cause trouble. They could screw up a simple situation so that something that seemed really easy could become really hard. Such was the case with me and my buddy Seymour. Seymour and I had fish camps across the river from each other on the Yukon and we fished the same eddy near a big bluff on the river.

It was August. King salmon season was in July and by mid-August there were no fish in the river. Chum salmon were still a couple of weeks off and you didn't want to shoot a moose for a long time yet. Seymour and I wanted a good piece of meat, though, so we took off in a canoe to go hunting for bear. We had five dogs along with us when we headed down to the Kandik River. We climbed up on bluffs and looked around. We had two guns with us. I had my big gun, the .243, and Seymour had his .22 because we had to feed the dogs, too. We were shooting squirrels for the dogs. We had a net in the water and we were catching pike. We spent a couple days down there but didn't find a bear, so we headed back up the river. We didn't have a motor, so we were lining the canoe up the bank. On good stretches of the bank, we'd hook the dogs up to pull us. Two dogs can pull a canoe just fine. So we were sitting in this canoe cruising up the river with our dogs when Seymour and I spotted a bear. It was in the river, maybe a quarter mile upstream from us. It had taken off from our side of the river and was swimming over to the other bank. We figured to let it swim most of the way across and paddle over to shoot it when it climbed out on the other side.

The river at that spot was about 500 yards wide and the bear was only partway across. He had a long way to go. We pulled into shore, got out, took our dogs out of their harnesses, and were talking in low tones and crouching down. We didn't want this bear to see us. Those dogs, though, were really great at reading body language. They were a lot better than any of us at it. They knew something was up, but they don't know what, so they were all being hypervigilant. We really didn't want them to see this bear, because they could alert it to our presence, or worse, swim after it and get into a battle midstream, which would be a terrible mess for numerous reasons.

We knew *they* knew something was up, so we were intentionally aiming our rifles downriver because usually when we pointed our rifles at something, all the dogs knew something was gonna die over there and they would get all excited about it. Unfortunately, our dogs weren't falling for this sham. They were all looking upriver because they knew that was where we were first looking when we stopped. We had this one dog who would watch jets moving across the sky. He had great eyesight and he spotted that bear out in the river. It was still 300 yards upstream from us and about 150 yards out in the river. So this dog took off running and all the other dogs took off after him, roaring up the bank. At that point the dogs might not even have known it was a bear. They might have thought it was a beaver, and they loved chasing beavers in the water. Seymour and I were going, "This is not good! This is just not good!" Suddenly this situation was not as simple as it had been a moment ago.

The dogs got up to where they were even with the bear on the shore. We were crossing our fingers. Maybe they wouldn't make noise because the bear still didn't see them. But no, they barked at him, so the bear turned around, lifted his nose into the air, trying to get wind of this new threat, but couldn't. Finally the bear could see the dogs and he's thinking, "Oh, no! There's a pack of wolves over there! I'm not going back to that side." So he turned back around and continued his journey across the river. Then all the dogs jumped into the river and started swimming out to him.

Seymour and I were saying, "This is not good at all!" because we had no idea what was gonna happen when those dogs caught the bear. Dogs swim a lot faster than bears do. They were going to catch him out in the middle of the river. We didn't know how big the bear was—all we could see was his head. So we were starting to freak out a little bit, but Seymour and I were not indecisive people. We were used to making decisions, and sometimes they had to be split-second decisions. So we thought, "Well, we can shoot the bear from here but then the bear is going to sink because bears don't float in the river." A lot of animals float in water, but bears sink and we were not gonna be able to live with ourselves if we shot the bear only to waste the meat.

So Seymour had this idea. He said, "Listen, you've got the big gun. You get in the front of the canoe and I'll get in the back. We'll paddle out there and beat the dogs to the bear. Right when we are just about on him, you shoot him and then grab him."

Right . . . But I was in my early twenties and Seymour was older than me, so I said, "Okay, that sounds like our best option as far as I can see."

We got in the canoe and went roaring out there, paddling with everything we had, and we passed the dogs. We got to the bear about two boat lengths ahead of the dogs. I popped the bear right in the head with the rifle and reached down immediately and grabbed him because he was about six feet in front of me when I shot him. He had already rolled forward and was on his way down. I grabbed him by the fur, right in front of the tail. We were still moving really fast and he was like a sea anchor at that point, so he nearly pulled me out of the canoe. As the canoe came to a sudden stop, the bear's nerves started going, so his legs were kicking and I was hanging onto him with my arm stretched out. Then the dogs caught up with us . . . The dogs jumped on this bear and started biting him and shaking. They were in a frenzy. I was afraid they were gonna bite my hand or pull the bear loose and he would sink and we'd lose him. I grabbed a paddle and started whacking at the dogs with one hand while holding onto the bear with the other. Meanwhile Seymour was laughing in the back of the canoe. There really wasn't anything else he could do about it because if he came to the front of the canoe, we'd flip it. So he couldn't do anything but laugh while I tried to fend the dogs off with the paddle.

Finally I "persuaded" the dogs to give me a little bit of space and they backed off. Seymour and I looked at each other and said, in amazement, "We got him!" You know, that was pretty amazing! We tried to pull him into the canoe but that didn't work because he was too big. So we tied him onto the side of the canoe and paddled to shore, kind of like the big marlin in *The Old Man and the Sea*. We lost about a mile of ground floating downriver as we struggled to get to shore. We dragged him up on the beach. He was about a 250-pound, cinnamon-phase black bear; they have a reddish fur on them. He had fattened up really nice eating berries for a while, so it was a tremendous piece of meat we were able to get . . . despite the dogs.

In retrospect, there were probably a couple things that could have gone wrong with that deal. I certainly wouldn't recommend it, but most of the time out in the woods things worked out for us. That's just the way it was.

Murphy's Law

KAITI OTT

Kaiti was like a gift to Dark Winter Nights *from the gods of storytelling. I met her at a storytelling class I was teaching and was thrilled when I found out she had a wonderful story about the hazards of doing science in the far reaches of Alaska. Not only that, but she went on to serve as a valuable member of our executive producer team for several years. It doesn't get any better than that for us at* Dark Winter Nights. *She shared this story at our April 2016 live event in Fairbanks.—Rob Prince*

This story takes place in the summer of 2006 in Prince William Sound, a beautiful coastal rainforest. We were on a remote island called Knight Island. It's about three and a half hours by small boat, in good weather, from Whittier, Alaska. We were there for a long time, about three and a half months, we had a pretty substantial field camp. We had multiple tent platforms, a weather port for cooking and drying our gear, and a fuel cache, and we had installed a really robust mooring for our boat. The boat we used for day-to-day work was a little seventeen-foot Boston Whaler. These boats are perfectly suited for doing fieldwork out in the Sound. They're really reliable . . . they float really well, and the boat we had that year was brand-new. It was top of the line, right off the assembly line. We were able to afford this boat because my advisor was particularly good at writing grants, and she wrote a grant specifically for this vessel, so it represented a significant chunk of our research budget. It was also really important to her sentimentally because it was named after her dearly departed dog, Gaia, who had spent several field seasons in the Sound with my advisor.

We had about half a dozen people in camp with us at any given time, coming and going, but there were several of us who were there for the whole field season. We had my advisor, her current dog, me, and another graduate student who was studying botany. For the purposes of this story I'm going to call him Murphy. That's an appropriate name because he was incredibly accident-prone. I'm not saying that to be mean or to poke fun at him. He's now an accomplished professional. But even he would admit that he was super accident-prone. Anything he got involved in kind of went south in a hurry. For example, one day as he was walking along in the forest, entering data in his field notebook, he walked off a fifteen-foot cliff. That was kind of a big deal, because we were a long way away from medical services. Luckily he walked away with just a sprained ankle, but it could have been a lot worse. Another day, as he was crashing through some understory on-site, the branches he was holding back slipped out of his grasp, whipping back and hitting him in the face. They actually tore his cornea, which was incredibly painful. He had to be medevaced to Anchorage for that one, and then he had the honor of wearing an eye patch for more than a month . . . But he recovered from that as well. So he was accident-prone, but he tried really hard.

There were a few things in camp he struggled with, like starting the fuel stove in the cook tent or gathering fresh water for drinking or . . . tying up the boat. We used a bowline knot. The bowline knot is fantastic. It's easy to tie and it's easy to untie, even after you've put a lot of tension on it. We all had to learn how to tie this knot, and demonstrate to our advisor that we could do it proficiently before she would let us tie up the boat. For whatever reason, Murphy just couldn't figure out the bowline. Our advisor taught him, we coached him, you could actually *sit with him* and guide his hands through the motions—and then you'd step away and say, "Okay, your turn," and his knot would fall apart. It was kind of frustrating for him, but it didn't really matter because the rest of us could step in and do it for him. We knew he was trying really hard, that was obvious, so it wasn't a big deal.

This being Alaska, we were used to all kinds of weather. Occasionally, we would have "weather days," or small craft advisories, when we wouldn't be able to work. We'd be stuck in camp, just staying in the cook tent all day. But there was one storm in particular that was really memorable—a gale warning. Those are fairly uncommon inside the Sound because it's pretty protected. We knew this storm was coming because we'd been listening to the marine radio, and it was forecast to hit overnight, then continue for a day or so beyond that. So as we were coming back to camp that day, we knew we had to batten down the hatches for this storm. So we hit the beach and everyone just scattered: one person grabbing gear and storing it under the weather port, another taking stuff off of lines and putting it away safe. We all had numerous chores that we just had to get done. But we finished and were able to go back to the cook tent, have a nice hot meal, and relax. As the storm started to pick up, we just visited in the cook tent, told stories, played cards, and ate snack food. We knew we didn't have to go to work the next day because it was going to be a really bad weather day.

So we stayed up pretty late; it was probably 1:30 a.m. before we turned in. As we were heading off to our tents, we looked out at the beach and squinted into the rain and the wind. We could see the *Gaia* riding high. She was still out there, so that was good. I crawled into my sleeping bag and settled down for the night, listening to the waves crashing on the beach. Then I thought I heard something: was that something hitting the beach? "Nah," I thought. "I'm sure everything's fine . . ." But my mind had started running and couldn't stop. "I hope the boat's okay . . . who tied up the boat today?" And then it suddenly dawned on me . . . "Oh, my gosh! It was Murphy! Murphy tied up the boat today!" I don't know how it had escaped our collective attention, but when we all got back to camp, fixated on accomplishing so many tasks before the storm hit, nobody raised a red flag when he volunteered to tie up the boat.

So I was thinking, "Oh, God! What do I do!? . . . Well, maybe it's fine. She was still on the mooring when we went to bed, so she's not going anywhere . . . I should just try to go to sleep. It's fine . . . Just sleep." But the more I heard the waves crashing and imagined the sounds of things hitting the beach, the more I imagined the *Gaia* getting wrecked. And I started thinking that in the morning, if the *Gaia* was either gone or wrecked against the beach, I wouldn't be able to look my advisor in the eye and admit I'd realized there was a potentially *huge* problem but did nothing about it. So, I begrudgingly realized that the only way I was going to get any sleep was to go check that knot.

So I hauled myself out of bed, put on my cold clammy rain gear and my Xtratufs, and trudged down the trail to the beach, grabbing my life vest along the way. The *Gaia* was still there. "Well, that's good!" I thought in relief. The tide was really high, so that was good too, meaning I wouldn't have to drag the dinghy too far to get to the water. In order to ferry ourselves from shore to the *Gaia*, we would use this little inflatable dinghy. It was like a one-person inner tube with a plywood floor and oar locks.

It took awhile for me to launch the little dinghy into the waves and the gale winds, but eventually I reached the *Gaia*. I crawled over the *Gaia*'s rail, knowing I was only going to be there for about thirty seconds, tops, because I was just going to check this knot. So I really quickly tied the dinghy to the rail with a half hitch. I ran to the *Gaia*'s bow, pulled up the bowline, fixed my headlamp on that knot . . . and it was perfect. There was *nothing* wrong with that knot. It was textbook. I don't know how he did it, but he did. So I was kind of incredulous for a minute. "Cool! Okay, wow . . . good for him!" I dropped the knot and turned around just in time to see the line on the dinghy unravel and go—*fwoop!*—right off the rail.

"Oh . . . that's ironic!" I thought. "But this is *bad*, because there goes my ride to shore." At that moment I really didn't have a whole lot of options. I could swim for it, but that would be really stupid because it was right in the middle of a gale, dark, and nobody knew I was out there. Or I could wait overnight for somebody to get the dinghy and rescue me. Or . . . I could try to catch the dingy with the *Gaia*. I decided that was my best option, but I'd have to do it fast. This was close to the beach, but it wasn't a sandy, soft beach, it was a rocky, bouldery beach. Any boat pushed against this beach was going to be destroyed in short order. So I didn't have a whole lot of time to catch the dinghy before it got into shallow water where I couldn't follow it.

I ran to the center console of the boat. Boston Whalers are built such that you stand up and steer from the center, and when you turn the ignition switch, it makes a high-pitched *beeeeep!* The *Gaia* started right up. I ran to the bow and untied that perfect bowline knot, then ran back to the console, threw it in gear, and whipped the *Gaia* around toward shore. Then I started the most intense medium-speed chase you've ever seen.

I didn't have a whole lot of freeboard. The waves were kind of throwing off my mental map of what the shoreline looked like and of how much draft I actually had, but I knew it wasn't much. So I was chasing after this dinghy, but I didn't want my momentum to carry me beyond where I could actually stop and thus run me into the rocks. I knew I was getting shallow, and I was anticipating that at any moment I'd feel the hull ground out. So I raised the prop about halfway, because I didn't want to bust the prop on the bottom, but when I did that, it also meant I didn't have as much power for maneuverability. So the prop was half raised and I was *slowly* chasing after the dinghy but I just knew I was going to wreck this boat.

But eventually, I somehow caught up to the dinghy and bumped it with the nose of the *Gaia*. So I ran to the bow, grabbed the line of the dinghy, and ran back to the console. Now my only option was to back straight up the way I had come. If I tried to do a U-turn, I would be broadside to the waves and that would immediately push me against the rocks and it would all be over in a heartbeat. But I was backing straight into the huge waves, and I didn't have as much power from my half-raised prop, so it was an extremely slow process. Of course, now that I was backing straight into them, the waves were coming right over the transom and filling the boat with seawater.

But it was working! Very slowly, but it was working!

Eventually I managed to limp back into deeper water and lower the prop, turn around, and head back out to the buoy. As I was tying up the *Gaia*, I realized I'd better spend a little time bilging all of this seawater out as there was probably about a foot of water in the hull of the *Gaia*, and that's a lot of volume. I breathed a sigh of relief, thinking, "Thank God, nobody got hurt. I didn't destroy our boat . . . and nobody knows this happened!"

When I finished bilging, I jumped back in the dinghy, and as I was thankfully rowing back to shore, I noticed there was somebody standing on the beach. And I could kind of tell from their posture that they were not happy . . .

It was my advisor. My displeased advisor . . . When I started the engine and the ignition went *beeeeep*, her dog heard it and alerted her that something was wrong. She thought it was maybe a bear in camp, but it turned out that her graduate student was taking the boat for a joy ride in the middle of a gale in the shallow end.

So she came out at 2:00 in the morning in her rain gear to see this entire circus unfold. She had *a lot* of questions for me. She was upset, and understandably so. First of all, she was the primary investigator on this study. She was responsible for everyone's safety. I definitely should have told somebody what I was going to do. Second, she was responsible for an incredibly complex budget and logistical plan, and the crux of that plan was this boat. If this boat weren't operational, then we would have wasted tons of money and lots of people's time. So if something were to happen to it, it would have been really bad.

To this day, Murphy doesn't know that I doubted him that much, and I would be really embarrassed if he found out. But I also learned a few things from this experience. The first is to always, *no matter what*, use the appropriate knot for the situation. Second, maybe don't be so quick to write somebody off if they make a mistake or two, because they just might come back to surprise you like Murphy did.